QUICK-RESPONSE E...

BOOK 1

LEARN ENGLISH WITH

100

PHRASAL VERBS

English Conversation Dialogues for ESL and EFL Teachers, Students, and Self-Study Learners

ELEANOR EBY

Cover design and interior design by J. Her

ISBN 979-8-9893179-6-7

FJORDHILL
PRESS
P.O. Box 51, Hilbert WI 54129

Contact the author at: quickresponseenglish@gmail.com

TABLE OF CONTENTS

Introduction

Phrasal verbs can be difficult and confusing, but they are essential to speaking English naturally and fluently. Perhaps you're an English learner and you've memorized many phrasal verbs, but you have trouble using them quickly and smoothly in real conversation. Perhaps you're an ESL/EFL teacher and you want your students to learn phrasal verbs in context, or you're just looking for a way to enrich your conversation lessons and encourage more speaking. Whether you're an English learner preparing for the TOEIC/TOEFL exams, or you're a teacher looking for no-prep activities to get your students talking, this book is for you.

In my nearly 20 years of teaching EFL and ESL, I've found that most phrasal verb books focus on input (reading, memorizing) rather than output (speaking). You can find many books with dictionary definitions, vocabulary lists to memorize, and fill-in-the-blank exercises, but those books aren't likely to improve your speaking confidence or "liven up" your English lessons. This book is different.

This is a speaking-focused book, providing the framework for English learners to spend time speaking aloud. Each activity has the quick, back-and-forth dynamic of real conversation to help learners gain confidence, not only with phrasal verbs, but also with English speaking in general. I've used these fun and engaging activities with my own students over the years, and students familiar with these activities often request them again during conversation lessons.

In this book, you'll find 100 phrasal verbs divided into 10 chapters with four detailed speaking activities per chapter, each following a specific pattern. There are over 800 sentences to be spoken aloud in short dialogues, which can be expanded into longer conversations. Each activity includes Shadowing, Independent Responses, and opportunities to lengthen conversations, as well as self-study directions for learning outside of lessons.

With this book, my goal is that you will be able to:

1. Practice common phrasal verbs in context while speaking aloud.

2. Improve smoothness, confidence, and response time through repetition of full sentences and independent responses (responding without looking at the text).

3. Demonstrate understanding by adding your own context in short conversations surrounding each phrasal verb. **And above all, have fun and find your voice with Quick-Response English!**

About the Author: Eleanor Eby

As of 2023, Eleanor Eby has been teaching English for nearly 20 years. After graduating with a degree in English from the University of Wisconsin, she taught EFL in Japan to adult students of all levels (Business English and conversation). When she returned to the U.S., she worked for a community college in the Midwest, teaching ESL classes to adult English learners and Written Composition classes to first-year college students. Eleanor currently teaches English online to adult students of all levels in the U.S., Japan, Taiwan, South Korea, China, Hong Kong, Germany, France, Spain, and the U.K.

Not Just Vocabulary Study: Although this book focuses on detailed practice with phrasal verbs, these activities can simply be used to add some structure to conversation lessons for students who need or want more structure. Phrasal verb acquisition is just a bonus in that situation, and the phrasal verbs become a springboard for more conversation. I've found that it's quite effective to do the following: start the lesson with small talk, move into some discussion questions, and spend the last part of the lesson doing one of the activities in this book. Students come away energized by the quick dialogues and also with some concrete speaking patterns to review and practice after the lesson.

Student Levels: This book has been used with students of the following levels (Cambridge English levels): B1 (Intermediate), B2 (Upper-Intermediate), and C1 (Advanced). Less confident B1 students may wish to read the Part A sentences while repeating after you, before moving forward with true shadowing. For more confident B2 students, simply follow the instructions in each activity. For C1 students, shadowing may not be necessary unless the student needs pronunciation practice. C1 students may benefit the most from the third and fourth activities in each chapter, especially continuing longer conversations while focusing on smoothness, speed, and pronunciation.

Shadowing: Every activity starts with shadowing, and this is a great opportunity to focus on listening, pronunciation, rhythm, speed, and liaisons, and give your students corrections as needed.

Speaking Without Looking at the Text: Encourage your students to look away from the text as much as possible, as described in the instructions. The goal at the end of each exercise is to have your student close the book and be able to do the exercise smoothly and confidently without looking at any text.

In All the Activities: The phrasal verbs are given in "dictionary form," which means students may need to change the verb to match the sentence and the pattern of the exercise (singular/plural, past/present/future). For example, "pick up" --> "He pick<u>s</u> up . . . / He pick<u>ed</u> up . . .", etc.

Structure and Following Language Patterns: Many phrasal verbs have multiple meanings, and I've tried to include the most common meanings in this book, but for the sake of brevity, I didn't include every possible meaning of every phrasal verb. In the answer keys, I've included the most natural or most common answers. Students may occasionally come up with other correct answers, and that's fine! However, be sure students' answers still follow the basic pattern of the activity, since learning language patterns improves speed and confidence. There's usually no need to explain these patterns to students because they quickly get a feel for the pattern by practicing the examples and doing shadowing.

Self-Study and Homework: Every activity includes "Self-Study" instructions, which your students can use before a lesson or for review/homework after the lesson.

Classroom Setting: Because of the increased popularity of private online English lessons, the instructions in this book assume one-on-one learning. In a classroom setting or with multiple students, you may have students work on these exercises in pairs.

CHAPTER 1

1. figure out

2. put off

3. heat up

4. get together

5. throw away

6. come down with

7. look over

8. clean up

9. run into

10. take over

1.1 QUICK CHANGES
Quickly change regular sentences into phrasal-verb sentences

THE GOAL of this activity is to learn the meaning of each phrasal verb through context. Change the original sentence into a new, more natural sentence using the phrasal verb. Try to keep the sentences as similar as possible and change the phrasal verb form if necessary.

Step 1: Shadowing
Listen to your teacher read parts A and B aloud, and repeat each sentence without looking at the text (the teacher may use the answer key). If you need to glance at the text, use part A (below).

Step 2: Independent Response
Next, listen to your teacher read part A (phrasal verb and sentence), and create part B yourself without looking at the text. Repeat until you can speak smoothly.

EXAMPLE
get together . . . We meet at the café once a week.
A) "get together . . . We meet at the café once a week."
B) "We get together at the café once a week."

A)

1. figure out . . . I solve a lot of problems at work.

2. put off . . . We often postpone meetings when we're busy.

3. heat up . . . If we don't have time to cook, we can warm some food in the microwave.

4. get together . . . We meet at the café once a week.

5. throw away . . . She wants to discard her old clothes.

6. come down with . . . He catches a cold every winter.

7. look over . . . She carefully examines all her bank statements.

8. clean up . . . He's a messy cook, so he has to clean the kitchen after cooking.

9. run into . . . I'm worried that I will suddenly meet my old boss at the station.

10. take over . . . He's sick, so could you lead his presentation?

11. run into . . . The sidewalk is crowded, so please try not to hit people with your bike.

Step 3: "No Hint" and Extra Comment

Listen to your teacher read part A **without** the phrasal verb and create part B yourself, remembering the phrasal verb from context. Add an extra comment to make your answer longer, and repeat until you can speak smoothly.

EXAMPLE:
get together . . . We meet at the café once a week.
A) "We meet at the café once a week."
B) "We get together at the café once a week. We usually spend a few hours there."

Step 4: Continue the Conversation!

Do Step 3 again but continue a short, back-and-forth conversation with your teacher or language partner.

EXAMPLE:
get together . . . We meet at the café once a week.
A) "We meet at the café once a week."
B) "We get together at the café once a week. We usually spend a few hours there."
A) "Does that café have meals, or just snacks?"
B) "They have sandwiches and desserts. We usually eat too much!"

Self-Study

Step 1: Read the examples aloud to get used to the pattern, and then go to Step 2.

Step 2: Read part A aloud and then try to create part B without looking at the text. Check your answers with the answer key. Repeat until you can speak part B smoothly without looking at the text.

Step 3: Cover the phrasal verbs with your hand or a sheet of paper. Read part A aloud **without** the phrasal verb and then create part B without looking at the text. Try to remember each phrasal verb from context. Add an extra comment to make your answer longer.

Step 4: Do step 3 again but continue a short, back-and-forth imaginary conversation. Practice while speaking aloud.

1.2 QUICK ANSWERS
Answer questions quickly and naturally

THE GOAL of this activity is to give a quick, short answer using a phrasal verb in conversation. Use past tense and use "it/them" to keep your answer short and natural.

Step 1: Shadowing

Listen to your teacher read parts A and B aloud, and repeat each sentence without looking at the text (the teacher may use the answer key). If you need to glance at the text, use part A (below).

Step 2: Independent Response

Next, listen to your teacher read part A (phrasal verb and sentence), and create part B yourself without looking at the text. Repeat until you can speak smoothly.

EXAMPLE

come down with . . . Did she get the flu?
A) "come down with . . . Did she get the flu?"
B) "She came down with it."

A)

1. figure out . . . Did you discover how to create your own YouTube channel?

2. put off . . . Did they postpone their party?

3. heat up . . . Did he warm that cold soup before eating it?

4. get together . . . Did you and your uncle meet last week?

5. throw away . . . Did he discard his old laptop?

6. come down with . . . Did she get the flu?

7. look over . . . Did you take a look at the online schedule?

8. clean up . . . Did your son tidy his bedroom?

9. run into . . . Did you see our new clients at the conference?

10. take over . . . Did she take control of the project?

Step 3: "No Hint" and Extra Comment

Listen to your teacher read part A **without** the phrasal verb and create part B yourself, remembering the phrasal verb from context. Add an extra comment to make your answer longer, and repeat until you can speak smoothly.

EXAMPLE:

come down with . . . Did she get the flu?
A) "Did she get the flu?"
B) "She came down with it. She had a really high fever!"

Step 4: Continue the Conversation!

Do Step 3 again but continue a short, back-and-forth conversation with your teacher or language partner.

EXAMPLE:

come down with . . . Did she get the flu?
A) "Did she get the flu?"
B) "She came down with it. She had a really high fever!"
A) "That's too bad. How long was she sick?"
B) "She started feeling better after about a week."

Self-Study

Step 1: Read the examples aloud to get used to the pattern, and then go to Step 2.

Step 2: Read part A aloud and then try to create part B without looking at the text. Check your answers with the answer key. Repeat until you can speak part B smoothly without looking at the text.

Step 3: Cover the phrasal verbs with your hand or a sheet of paper. Read part A aloud **without** the phrasal verb and then create part B without looking at the text. Try to remember each phrasal verb from context. Add an extra comment to make your answer longer.

Step 4: Do step 3 again but continue a short, back-and-forth imaginary conversation. Practice while speaking aloud.

1.3 QUICK BUILDER
Quickly build more detailed answers

THE GOAL of this activity is to add more detail to your answer quickly with an extra verb. Follow the pattern (verb + to + phrasal verb) and create a past or future tense answer. Use "it/them" for a short, natural response.

Step 1: Shadowing

Listen to your teacher read parts A and B aloud, and repeat each sentence without looking at the text (the teacher may use the answer key). If you need to glance at the text, use part A (below).

Step 2: Independent Response

Next, listen to your teacher read part A (extra verb and sentence), and create part B yourself without looking at the text. Repeat until you can speak smoothly.

EXAMPLE

want . . . Is he going to put off the presentation?
A) "want . . . Is he going to put off the presentation?"
B) "He wants to put it off."

A)

1. try . . . Did she figure out the printer problem?

2. want . . . Is he going to put off the presentation?

3. forget . . . Did you heat up the pasta for dinner?

4. plan . . . Are they going to get together soon?

5. decide not . . . Did you throw away your old skis?

6. happen . . . Did he come down with the flu?

7. promise . . . Is she going to look over your resume?

8. decide . . . Did he clean up the living room?

9. happen . . . Did they run into her at the park?

10. agree . . . Did you take over the book club when your leader quit?

Step 3: "No Hint" and Extra Comment

Listen to your teacher read part A **without** the extra verb and create part B yourself, remembering the verb from before. Add an extra comment to make your answer longer, and repeat until you can speak smoothly.

> ### EXAMPLE:
> want . . . Is he going to put off the presentation?
> A) "Is he going to put off the presentation?"
> B) "He wants to put it off. Two of his team members are out sick."

Step 4: Continue the Conversation!

Do Step 3 again but continue a short, back-and-forth conversation with your teacher or language partner.

> ### EXAMPLE:
> want . . . Is he going to put off the presentation?
> A) "Is he going to put off the presentation?"
> B) "He wants to put it off. Two of his team members are out sick."
> A) "When will they be back?"
> B) "Probably next week. He's going to ask his manager about it."

Self-Study

Step 1: Read the examples aloud to get used to the pattern, and then go to Step 2.

Step 2: Read part A aloud and then try to create part B without looking at the text. Check your answers with the answer key. Repeat until you can speak part B smoothly without looking at the text.

Step 3: Cover the extra verbs with your hand or a sheet of paper. Read part A aloud **without** the extra verb and then create part B without looking at the text. Try to remember the verb from before. Add an extra comment to make your answer longer.

Step 4: Do step 3 again but continue a short, back-and-forth imaginary conversation. Practice while speaking aloud.

1.4 QUICK QUESTIONS
Quickly ask questions to keep the conversation going

THE GOAL of this activity is to improve your small-talk skills by quickly asking a relevant question to keep the conversation going. Remember, being good at small talk means being good at asking questions! Use "it/them" and create a past or future tense question to match the situation.

Step 1: Shadowing
Listen to your teacher read parts A and B aloud, and repeat each sentence without looking at the text (the teacher may use the answer key). If you need to glance at the text, use part A (below).

Step 2: Independent Response
Next, listen to your teacher read part A (phrasal verb and sentence), and create part B yourself without looking at the text. Repeat until you can speak smoothly.

EXAMPLE
run into . . . I wanted to see my old high school friend at the reunion.
A) "run into . . . I wanted to see my old high school friend at the reunion."
B) "Did you run into him?"

A)

1. figure out . . . He tried to find his way to the cafe.

2. put off . . . They want to postpone their wedding.

3. heat up . . . I drank the old coffee instead of making more.

4. get together . . . We want to spend time together next week.

5. throw away . . . I got rid of my old sofa.

6. come down with . . . He was worried his daughter would catch Covid.

7. look over . . . He wants her to check his resume.

8. clean up . . . She asked them to clean and organize the conference room.

9. run into . . . I wanted to see my old high school friend at the reunion.

10. take over . . . She might be in charge of the cooking class when our teacher retires.

Step 3: "No Hint"

Listen to your teacher read part A **without** the phrasal verb and create part B yourself, remembering the phrasal verb from context. Repeat until you can speak smoothly.

EXAMPLE:
run into . . . I wanted to see my old high school friend at the reunion.
A) "I wanted to see my old high school friend at the reunion."
B) "Did you run into him?"

Step 4: Continue the Conversation!

Do Step 3 again but continue a short, back-and-forth conversation with your teacher or language partner.

EXAMPLE:
run into . . . I wanted to see my old high school friend at the reunion.
A) "I wanted to see my old high school friend at the reunion."
B) "Did you run into him?"
A) "Yes, he was there with his wife and kids."
B) "Does he have a big family?"
A) "He has five kids!"

Self-Study

Step 1: Read the examples aloud to get used to the pattern, and then go to Step 2.

Step 2: Read part A aloud and then try to create part B without looking at the text. Check your answers with the answer key. Repeat until you can speak part B smoothly without looking at the text.

Step 3: Cover the phrasal verbs with your hand or a sheet of paper. Read part A aloud **without** the phrasal verb and then create part B without looking at the text. Try to remember each phrasal verb from context. Repeat until you can speak smoothly and without hesitation.

Step 4: Do step 3 again but continue a short, back-and-forth imaginary conversation. Practice while speaking aloud.

CHAPTER

1. give away

2. take care of

3. put away

4. ask over

5. go up

6. pick up

7. sleep in

8. put on

9. work on

10. hang out

QUICK CHANGES
Quickly change regular sentences into phrasal-verb sentences

THE GOAL of this activity is to learn the meaning of each phrasal verb through context. Change the original sentence into a new, more natural sentence using the phrasal verb. Try to keep the sentences as similar as possible and change the phrasal verb form if necessary.

Step 1: Shadowing

Listen to your teacher read parts A and B aloud, and repeat each sentence without looking at the text (the teacher may use the answer key). If you need to glance at the text, use part A (below).

Step 2: Independent Response

Next, listen to your teacher read part A (phrasal verb and sentence), and create part B yourself without looking at the text. Repeat until you can speak smoothly.

EXAMPLE
sleep in . . . I sleep late on Saturday mornings.
A) "sleep in . . . I sleep late on Saturday mornings."
B) "I sleep in on Saturday mornings."

A)

1. give away . . . She donates her old clothes to the secondhand shop.

2. take care of . . . When her brother travels, she cares for his dog.

3. put away . . . He always puts his clean laundry in the closet.

4. ask over . . . He invites his friends to his house every weekend.

5. go up . . . I hope food prices don't increase this year.

6. pick up . . . I usually get groceries after work.

7. sleep in . . . I sleep late on Saturday mornings.

8. put on . . . We need to dress in warm clothes before we go out in the blizzard.

9. work on . . . I should spend time doing my tax paperwork this month.

10. hang out . . . They usually spend time together at the park.

11. take care of . . . I don't have time, so can you handle that new project yourself?

12. pick up . . . He asked his brother to go and get the kids from school.

13. put on . . . She asked her son to clean up his books and place them on his shelf.

Step 3: "No Hint" and Extra Comment

Listen to your teacher read part A **without** the phrasal verb and create part B yourself, remembering the phrasal verb from context. Add an extra comment to make your answer longer, and repeat until you can speak smoothly.

EXAMPLE:

sleep in . . . I sleep late on Saturday mornings.
A) "I sleep late on Saturday mornings."
B) "I sleep in on Saturday mornings. My dog finally wakes me up."

Step 4: Continue the Conversation!

Do Step 3 again but continue a short, back-and-forth conversation with your teacher or language partner.

EXAMPLE:

sleep in . . . I sleep late on Saturday mornings.
A) "I sleep late on Saturday mornings."
B) "I sleep in on Saturday mornings. My dog finally wakes me up."
A) "What does your dog do?"
B) "He jumps on my bed and licks my face."

Self-Study

Step 1: Read the examples aloud to get used to the pattern, and then go to Step 2.

Step 2: Read part A aloud and then try to create part B without looking at the text. Check your answers with the answer key. Repeat until you can speak part B smoothly without looking at the text.

Step 3: Cover the phrasal verbs with your hand or a sheet of paper. Read part A aloud **without** the phrasal verb and then create part B without looking at the text. Try to remember each phrasal verb from context. Add an extra comment to make your answer longer.

Step 4: Do step 3 again but continue a short, back-and-forth imaginary conversation. Practice while speaking aloud.

2.2 QUICK ANSWERS
Answer questions quickly and naturally

THE GOAL of this activity is to give a quick, short answer using a phrasal verb in conversation. Use past tense and use "it/them" to keep your answer short and natural.

Step 1: Shadowing
Listen to your teacher read parts A and B aloud, and repeat each sentence without looking at the text (the teacher may use the answer key). If you need to glance at the text, use part A (below).

Step 2: Independent Response
Next, listen to your teacher read part A (phrasal verb and sentence), and create part B yourself without looking at the text. Repeat until you can speak smoothly.

EXAMPLE
pick up . . . Did he get milk on his way home?
A) "pick up . . . Did he get milk on his way home?"
B) "He picked it up."

A)

1. give away . . . Did you give your prize money to someone else after the contest?

2. take care of . . . Did he look after the kids?

3. put away . . . Did she put the car in the garage?

4. ask over . . . Did you invite your aunt to your house?

5. go up . . . Did your rent increase last year?

6. pick up . . . Did he get milk on his way home?

7. sleep in . . . Did she sleep late this morning?

8. put on . . . Did you wear your motorcycle helmet?

9. work on . . . Did you practice your speech?

10. hang out . . . Did they spend time at the beach?

Step 3: "No Hint" and Extra Comment

Listen to your teacher read part A **without** the phrasal verb and create part B yourself, remembering the phrasal verb from context. Add an extra comment to make your answer longer, and repeat until you can speak smoothly.

EXAMPLE:
pick up . . . Did he get milk on his way home?
A) "Did he get milk on his way home?"
B) "He picked it up. His daughter texted him to remind him."

Step 4: Continue the Conversation!

Do Step 3 again but continue a short, back-and-forth conversation with your teacher or language partner.

EXAMPLE:
pick up . . . Did he get milk on his way home?
A) "Did he get milk on his way home?"
B) "He picked it up. His daughter texted him to remind him."
A) "Does he usually go to the grocery store after work?"
B) "Yeah, there's a grocery store close to his office."

Self-Study

Step 1: Read the examples aloud to get used to the pattern, and then go to Step 2.

Step 2: Read part A aloud and then try to create part B without looking at the text. Check your answers with the answer key. Repeat until you can speak part B smoothly without looking at the text.

Step 3: Cover the phrasal verbs with your hand or a sheet of paper. Read part A aloud **without** the phrasal verb and then create part B without looking at the text. Try to remember each phrasal verb from context. Add an extra comment to make your answer longer.

Step 4: Do step 3 again but continue a short, back-and-forth imaginary conversation. Practice while speaking aloud.

THE GOAL of this activity is to add more detail to your answer quickly with an extra verb. Follow the pattern (verb + to + phrasal verb) and create a past or future tense answer. Use "it/them" for a short, natural response.

Step 1: Shadowing

Listen to your teacher read parts A and B aloud, and repeat each sentence without looking at the text (the teacher may use the answer key). If you need to glance at the text, use part A (below).

Step 2: Independent Response

Next, listen to your teacher read part A (extra verb and sentence), and create part B yourself without looking at the text. Repeat until you can speak smoothly.

EXAMPLE

decide not . . . Did he pick up groceries?
A) "decide not . . . Did he pick up groceries?"
B) "He decided not to pick them up."

A)

1. decide . . . Did she give away those concert tickets?

2. promise . . . Is he going to take care of this mess?

3. forget . . . Did you put away your bike?

4. plan . . . Are they going to ask their neighbors over?

5. happen . . . Did his tuition go up?

6. decide not . . . Did he pick up groceries?

7. hope . . . Is she going to sleep in this weekend?

8. forget . . . Did she put on sunscreen at the beach?

9. agree . . . Did they work on their company's website design?

10. want . . . Are you going to hang out with your coworkers at the party?

Step 3: "No Hint" and Extra Comment

Listen to your teacher read part A **without** the extra verb and create part B yourself, remembering the verb from before. Add an extra comment to make your answer longer, and repeat until you can speak smoothly.

EXAMPLE:

decide not . . . Did he pick up groceries?
A) "Did he pick up groceries?"
B) "He decided not to pick them up. He's planning to go to Costco tomorrow instead."

Step 4: Continue the Conversation!

Do Step 3 again but continue a short, back-and-forth conversation with your teacher or language partner.

EXAMPLE:

decide not . . . Did he pick up groceries?
A) "Did he pick up groceries?"
B) "He decided not to pick them up. He's planning to go to Costco tomorrow instead."
A) "Does he buy a lot of stuff at Costco?"
B) "He usually buys too much!"

Self-Study

Step 1: Read the examples aloud to get used to the pattern, and then go to Step 2.

Step 2: Read part A aloud and then try to create part B without looking at the text. Check your answers with the answer key. Repeat until you can speak part B smoothly without looking at the text.

Step 3: Cover the extra verbs with your hand or a sheet of paper. Read part A aloud **without** the extra verb and then create part B without looking at the text. Try to remember the verb from before. Add an extra comment to make your answer longer.

Step 4: Do step 3 again but continue a short, back-and-forth imaginary conversation. Practice while speaking aloud.

Quickly ask questions to keep the conversation going

THE GOAL of this activity is to improve your small-talk skills by quickly asking a relevant question to keep the conversation going. Remember, being good at small talk means being good at asking questions! Use "it/them" and create a past or future tense question to match the situation.

Step 1: Shadowing

Listen to your teacher read parts A and B aloud, and repeat each sentence without looking at the text (the teacher may use the answer key). If you need to glance at the text, use part A (below).

Step 2: Independent Response

Next, listen to your teacher read part A (phrasal verb and sentence), and create part B yourself without looking at the text. Repeat until you can speak smoothly.

EXAMPLE

take care of . . . My neighbor asked me to look after her cat last weekend.
A) "take care of . . . My neighbor asked me to look after her cat last weekend."
B) "Did you take care of it?"

A)

1. give away . . . I'm not going to keep those movie tickets.

2. take care of . . . My neighbor asked me to look after her cat last weekend.

3. put away . . . She asked her son to put the lawnmower in the garage.

4. ask over . . . I wanted to invite my friends to my house for dinner.

5. go up . . . I was worried my son's fever would get higher.

6. pick up . . . She asked him to come and get her from the station.

7. sleep in . . . I hope to get lots of sleep this weekend.

8. put on . . . He told his daughter to wear her seatbelt on her road trip.

9. work on . . . I need to practice and improve my English this year.

10. hang out . . . They wanted to spend time together last Sunday.

Step 3: "No Hint"

Listen to your teacher read part A **without** the phrasal verb and create part B yourself, remembering the phrasal verb from context. Repeat until you can speak smoothly.

EXAMPLE:

take care of . . . My neighbor asked me to look after her cat last weekend.
A) "My neighbor asked me to look after her cat last weekend."
B) "Did you take care of it?"

Step 4: Continue the Conversation!

Do Step 3 again but continue a short, back-and-forth conversation with your teacher or language partner.

EXAMPLE:

take care of . . . My neighbor asked me to look after her cat last weekend.
A) "My neighbor asked me to look after her cat last weekend."
B) "Did you take care of it?"
A) "Yes, I love her cat!"
B) "Do you have any cats of your own?"
A) "No, but I had so much fun taking care of her cat, now I'm considering getting one."

Self-Study

Step 1: Read the examples aloud to get used to the pattern, and then go to Step 2.

Step 2: Read part A aloud and then try to create part B without looking at the text. Check your answers with the answer key. Repeat until you can speak part B smoothly without looking at the text.

Step 3: Cover the phrasal verbs with your hand or a sheet of paper. Read part A aloud **without** the phrasal verb and then create part B without looking at the text. Try to remember each phrasal verb from context. Repeat until you can speak smoothly and without hesitation.

Step 4: Do step 3 again but continue a short, back-and-forth imaginary conversation. Practice while speaking aloud.

CHAPTER

1. get rid of

2. look into

3. think over

4. work out

5. get along

6. try on

7. come back

8. turn on

9. look for

10. clean out

QUICK CHANGES
Quickly change regular sentences into phrasal-verb sentences

THE GOAL of this activity is to learn the meaning of each phrasal verb through context. Change the original sentence into a new, more natural sentence using the phrasal verb. Try to keep the sentences as similar as possible and change the phrasal verb form if necessary.

Step 1: Shadowing

Listen to your teacher read parts A and B aloud, and repeat each sentence without looking at the text (the teacher may use the answer key). If you need to glance at the text, use part A (below).

Step 2: Independent Response

Next, listen to your teacher read part A (phrasal verb and sentence), and create part B yourself without looking at the text. Repeat until you can speak smoothly.

EXAMPLE

get along with . . . I have a good relationship with my coworkers.
A) "get along with . . . I have a good relationship with my coworkers."
B) "I get along with my coworkers."

A)

1. get rid of . . . She often deletes the old photos on her phone.

2. look into . . . The police investigate a lot of crimes every year.

3. think over . . . He thinks carefully about every decision.

4. work out . . . She solves a lot of interpersonal problems in the office.

5. get along with . . . I have a good relationship with my coworkers.

6. try on . . . I always put on jeans to check the fit before buying them.

7. come back . . . They always return from trips with too many souvenirs.

8. turn on . . . You should start the electric heater.

9. look for . . . Every morning I search for my glasses.

10. clean out . . . It's time to clean and remove things from your garage.

11. look into . . . I decided to find more information about art classes for my daughter.

Step 3: "No Hint" and Extra Comment

Listen to your teacher read part A **without** the phrasal verb and create part B yourself, remembering the phrasal verb from context. Add an extra comment to make your answer longer, and repeat until you can speak smoothly.

EXAMPLE:

get along with . . . I have a good relationship with my coworkers.
A) "I have a good relationship with my coworkers."
B) "I get along with my coworkers. Our office environment is pretty relaxed."

Step 4: Continue the Conversation!

Do Step 3 again but continue a short, back-and-forth conversation with your teacher or language partner.

EXAMPLE:

get along with . . . I have a good relationship with my coworkers.
A) "I have a good relationship with my coworkers."
B) "I get along with my coworkers. Our office environment is pretty relaxed."
A) "Do you hang out with your coworkers after work?"
B) "Not really. I think that's why we enjoy working together!"

Self-Study

Step 1: Read the examples aloud to get used to the pattern, and then go to Step 2.

Step 2: Read part A aloud and then try to create part B without looking at the text. Check your answers with the answer key. Repeat until you can speak part B smoothly without looking at the text.

Step 3: Cover the phrasal verbs with your hand or a sheet of paper. Read part A aloud **without** the phrasal verb and then create part B without looking at the text. Try to remember each phrasal verb from context. Add an extra comment to make your answer longer.

Step 4: Do step 3 again but continue a short, back-and-forth imaginary conversation. Practice while speaking aloud.

Answer questions quickly and naturally

THE GOAL of this activity is to give a quick, short answer using a phrasal verb in conversation. Use past tense and use "it/them" to keep your answer short and natural.

Step 1: Shadowing

Listen to your teacher read parts A and B aloud, and repeat each sentence without looking at the text (the teacher may use the answer key). If you need to glance at the text, use part A (below).

Step 2: Independent Response

Next, listen to your teacher read part A (phrasal verb and sentence), and create part B yourself without looking at the text. Repeat until you can speak smoothly.

EXAMPLE
try on . . . Did he put on those ski boots to check the fit?
A) "try on . . . Did he put on those ski boots to check the fit?"
B) "He tried them on."

A)

1. get rid of . . . Did she throw away the receipt?

2. look into . . . Did they investigate their Wi-Fi problem?

3. think over . . . Did he think carefully about the job offer?

4. work out . . . Did you fix your schedule conflict?

5. get along with . . . Did you enjoy working with your new colleague?

6. try on . . . Did he put on those ski boots to check the fit?

7. come back . . . Did they already return from their trip?

8. turn on . . . Did you start up your computer?

9. look for . . . Did she search for her phone?

10. clean out . . . Did they clean and remove things from their office?

Step 3: "No Hint" and Extra Comment

Listen to your teacher read part A **without** the phrasal verb and create part B yourself, remembering the phrasal verb from context. Add an extra comment to make your answer longer, and repeat until you can speak smoothly.

EXAMPLE:

try on . . . Did he put on those ski boots to check the fit?
A) "Did he put on those ski boots to check the fit?"
B) "He tried them on. They're really expensive, so he wants to make sure they fit well."

Step 4: Continue the Conversation!

Do Step 3 again but continue a short, back-and-forth conversation with your teacher or language partner.

EXAMPLE:

try on . . . Did he put on those ski boots to check the fit?
A) "Did he put on those ski boots to check the fit?"
B) "He tried them on. They're really expensive, so he wants to make sure they fit well."
A) "Does he go skiing a lot?"
B) "Almost every weekend!"

Self-Study

Step 1: Read the examples aloud to get used to the pattern, and then go to Step 2.

Step 2: Read part A aloud and then try to create part B without looking at the text. Check your answers with the answer key. Repeat until you can speak part B smoothly without looking at the text.

Step 3: Cover the phrasal verbs with your hand or a sheet of paper. Read part A aloud **without** the phrasal verb and then create part B without looking at the text. Try to remember each phrasal verb from context. Add an extra comment to make your answer longer.

Step 4: Do step 3 again but continue a short, back-and-forth imaginary conversation. Practice while speaking aloud.

3.3 QUICK BUILDER
Quickly build more detailed answers

THE GOAL of this activity is to add more detail to your answer quickly with an extra verb. Follow the pattern (verb + to + phrasal verb) and create a past or future tense answer. Use "it/them" for a short, natural response.

Step 1: Shadowing

Listen to your teacher read parts A and B aloud, and repeat each sentence without looking at the text (the teacher may use the answer key). If you need to glance at the text, use part A (below).

Step 2: Independent Response

Next, listen to your teacher read part A (extra verb and sentence), and create part B yourself without looking at the text. Repeat until you can speak smoothly.

EXAMPLE
hope . . . Are they going to work out a time to meet?
A) "hope . . . Are they going to work out a time to meet?"
B) "They hope to work it out."

A)

1. decide . . . Did you get rid of the leftover food in your fridge?

2. agree . . . Did she look into our company's website issue?

3. promise . . . Are you going to think over my YouTube idea?

4. hope . . . Are they going to work out a time to meet?

5. seem . . . Did he get along with his homestay family?

6. decide not . . . Did he try on that expensive leather jacket?

7. hope . . . Are they going to come back to Japan?

8. forget . . . Did she turn on her home alarm system?

9. remember . . . Did he look for that important email from his boss?

10. plan . . . Are you going to clean out your car this weekend?

Step 3: "No Hint" and Extra Comment

Listen to your teacher read part A **without** the extra verb and create part B yourself, remembering the verb from before. Add an extra comment to make your answer longer, and repeat until you can speak smoothly.

EXAMPLE:
hope . . . Are they going to work out a time to meet?
A) "Are they going to work out a time to meet?"
B) "They hope to work it out. It might be tough since they're both busy."

Step 4: Continue the Conversation!

Do Step 3 again but continue a short, back-and-forth conversation with your teacher or language partner.

EXAMPLE:
hope . . . Are they going to work out a time to meet?
A) "Are they going to work out a time to meet?"
B) "They hope to work it out. It might be tough since they're both busy."
A) "Could they get together on the weekend?"
B) "Since it's work-related, they prefer to meet during the work week."

Self-Study

Step 1: Read the examples aloud to get used to the pattern, and then go to Step 2.

Step 2: Read part A aloud and then try to create part B without looking at the text. Check your answers with the answer key. Repeat until you can speak part B smoothly without looking at the text.

Step 3: Cover the extra verbs with your hand or a sheet of paper. Read part A aloud **without** the extra verb and then create part B without looking at the text. Try to remember the verb from before. Add an extra comment to make your answer longer.

Step 4: Do step 3 again but continue a short, back-and-forth imaginary conversation. Practice while speaking aloud.

THE GOAL of this activity is to improve your small-talk skills by quickly asking a relevant question to keep the conversation going. Remember, being good at small talk means being good at asking questions! Use "it/them" and create a past or future tense question to match the situation.

Step 1: Shadowing

Listen to your teacher read parts A and B aloud, and repeat each sentence without looking at the text (the teacher may use the answer key). If you need to glance at the text, use part A (below).

Step 2: Independent Response

Next, listen to your teacher read part A (phrasal verb and sentence), and create part B yourself without looking at the text. Repeat until you can speak smoothly.

EXAMPLE

get rid of . . . I don't want to keep my old car because it has too many issues.
A) "get rid of . . . I don't want to keep my old car because it has too many issues."
B) "Are you going to get rid of it?"

A)

1. get rid of . . . I don't want to keep my old car because it has too many issues.

2. look into . . . He wants to gather more information on that scholarship program.

3. think over . . . She can't decide whether or not to attend their wedding in Hawaii.

4. work out . . . They struggled to create a new social media plan for their company.

5. get along . . . I hope my dogs can spend time together next weekend without fighting.

6. try on . . . He looked at five different pairs of shoes at the store.

7. come back . . . She wanted to return home early from Paris.

8. turn on . . . He asked them to activate the alarm system when they left the house.

9. look for . . . She asked me to help her find her keys.

10. clean out . . . I should clean and remove everything from my kitchen cupboards.

Step 3: "No Hint"

Listen to your teacher read part A **without** the phrasal verb and create part B yourself, remembering the phrasal verb from context. Repeat until you can speak smoothly.

EXAMPLE:
get rid of . . . I don't want to keep my old car because it has too many issues.
A) "I don't want to keep my old car because it has too many issues."
B) "Are you going to get rid of it?"

Step 4: Continue the Conversation!

Do Step 3 again but continue a short, back-and-forth conversation with your teacher or language partner.

EXAMPLE:
get rid of . . . I don't want to keep my old car because it has too many issues.
A) "I don't want to keep my old car because it has too many issues."
B) "Are you going to get rid of it?"
A) "I think I'll trade it in at the car dealership."
B) "How much do you think it's worth?"
A) "I looked it up online, and I should be able to get at least $2,500 for it."

Self-Study

Step 1: Read the examples aloud to get used to the pattern, and then go to Step 2.

Step 2: Read part A aloud and then try to create part B without looking at the text. Check your answers with the answer key. Repeat until you can speak part B smoothly without looking at the text.

Step 3: Cover the phrasal verbs with your hand or a sheet of paper. Read part A aloud **without** the phrasal verb and then create part B without looking at the text. Try to remember each phrasal verb from context. Repeat until you can speak smoothly and without hesitation.

Step 4: Do step 3 again but continue a short, back-and-forth imaginary conversation. Practice while speaking aloud.

CHAPTER

4

1. look after

2. come up with

3. get over

4. fill out

5. try out

6. eat out

7. call back

8. shop around

9. start over

10. come across

THE GOAL of this activity is to learn the meaning of each phrasal verb through context. Change the original sentence into a new, more natural sentence using the phrasal verb. Try to keep the sentences as similar as possible and change the phrasal verb form if necessary.

Step 1: Shadowing

Listen to your teacher read parts A and B aloud, and repeat each sentence without looking at the text (the teacher may use the answer key). If you need to glance at the text, use part A (below).

Step 2: Independent Response

Next, listen to your teacher read part A (phrasal verb and sentence), and create part B yourself without looking at the text. Repeat until you can speak smoothly.

EXAMPLE

come up with . . . I usually think of good ideas in the morning.
A) "come up with . . . I usually think of good ideas in the morning."
B) "I usually come up with good ideas in the morning."

A)

1. look after . . . He needs to take care of his brother's kids.

2. come up with . . . I usually think of good ideas in the morning.

3. get over . . . She always recovers from colds quickly.

4. fill out . . . You need to complete this application by adding information.

5. try out . . . He wants to try using his new camera for the first time.

6. eat out . . . They eat at restaurants almost every night.

7. call back . . . She usually returns calls right away.

8. shop around . . . I always shop at multiple stores before buying anything.

9. start over . . . He doesn't like to start movies from the beginning again.

10. come across . . . She often encounters road construction in Chicago.

11. come up with . . . She creates a new recipe for gluten-free bread every week.

12. come across . . . I sometimes discover stray cats in my back yard.

Step 3: "No Hint" and Extra Comment

Listen to your teacher read part A **without** the phrasal verb and create part B yourself, remembering the phrasal verb from context. Add an extra comment to make your answer longer, and repeat until you can speak smoothly.

EXAMPLE:
come up with . . . I usually think of good ideas in the morning.
A) "I usually think of good ideas in the morning."
B) "I usually come up with good ideas in the morning. Especially while having my morning coffee."

Step 4: Continue the Conversation!

Do Step 3 again but continue a short, back-and-forth conversation with your teacher or language partner.

EXAMPLE:
come up with . . . I usually think of good ideas in the morning.
A) "I usually think of good ideas in the morning."
B) "I usually come up with good ideas in the morning. Especially while having my morning coffee."
A) "Are you a morning person?"
B) "No, but coffee wakes me up!"

Self-Study

Step 1: Read the examples aloud to get used to the pattern, and then go to Step 2.

Step 2: Read part A aloud and then try to create part B without looking at the text. Check your answers with the answer key. Repeat until you can speak part B smoothly without looking at the text.

Step 3: Cover the phrasal verbs with your hand or a sheet of paper. Read part A aloud **without** the phrasal verb and then create part B without looking at the text. Try to remember each phrasal verb from context. Add an extra comment to make your answer longer.

Step 4: Do step 3 again but continue a short, back-and-forth imaginary conversation. Practice while speaking aloud.

THE GOAL of this activity is to give a quick, short answer using a phrasal verb in conversation. Use past tense and use "it/them" to keep your answer short and natural.

Step 1: Shadowing

Listen to your teacher read parts A and B aloud, and repeat each sentence without looking at the text (the teacher may use the answer key). If you need to glance at the text, use part A (below).

Step 2: Independent Response

Next, listen to your teacher read part A (phrasal verb and sentence), and create part B yourself without looking at the text. Repeat until you can speak smoothly.

EXAMPLE

get over . . . Did he recover from losing his job?
A) "get over . . . Did he recover from losing his job?"
B) "He got over it."

A)

1. look after . . . Did he take care of his grandkids?

2. come up with . . . Did she create that new mobile app?

3. get over . . . Did he recover from losing his job?

4. fill out . . . Did she complete the online form?

5. try out . . . Did they test their new tent before their big camping trip?

6. eat out . . . Did she eat at a restaurant yesterday?

7. call back . . . Did they return his call?

8. shop around . . . Did he look in multiple stores?

9. start over . . . Did she start the project from the beginning again?

10. come across . . . Did you discover those old books in your attic?

Step 3: "No Hint" and Extra Comment

Listen to your teacher read part A **without** the phrasal verb and create part B yourself, remembering the phrasal verb from context. Add an extra comment to make your answer longer, and repeat until you can speak smoothly.

EXAMPLE:
get over . . . Did he recover from losing his job?
A) "Did he recover from losing his job?"
B) "He got over it. He found another job right away."

Step 4: Continue the Conversation!

Do Step 3 again but continue a short, back-and-forth conversation with your teacher or language partner.

EXAMPLE:
get over . . . Did he recover from losing his job?
A) "Did he recover from losing his job?"
B) "He got over it. He found another job right away."
A) "What field is he in?"
B) "He works in network security."

Self-Study

Step 1: Read the examples aloud to get used to the pattern, and then go to Step 2.

Step 2: Read part A aloud and then try to create part B without looking at the text. Check your answers with the answer key. Repeat until you can speak part B smoothly without looking at the text.

Step 3: Cover the phrasal verbs with your hand or a sheet of paper. Read part A aloud **without** the phrasal verb and then create part B without looking at the text. Try to remember each phrasal verb from context. Add an extra comment to make your answer longer.

Step 4: Do step 3 again but continue a short, back-and-forth imaginary conversation. Practice while speaking aloud.

4.3 QUICK BUILDER
Quickly build more detailed answers

THE GOAL of this activity is to add more detail to your answer quickly with an extra verb. Follow the pattern (verb + to + phrasal verb) and create a past or future tense answer. Use "it/them" for a short, natural response.

Step 1: Shadowing
Listen to your teacher read parts A and B aloud, and repeat each sentence without looking at the text (the teacher may use the answer key). If you need to glance at the text, use part A (below).

Step 2: Independent Response
Next, listen to your teacher read part A (extra verb and sentence), and create part B yourself without looking at the text. Repeat until you can speak smoothly.

EXAMPLE
plan . . . Are you going to start that novel over?
A) "plan . . . Are you going to start that novel over?"
B) "Yes, I plan to start it over."

A)

1. agree . . . Are you going to look after your friend's parrot?

2. forget . . . Did he come up with this week's video for his YouTube channel?

3. seem . . . Did they get over their argument?

4. decide not . . . Did you fill out the gym membership form?

5. want . . . Is she going to try out those new ice skates?

6. promise . . . Are they going to eat out with us this weekend?

7. remember . . . Did you call your mom back?

8. hope . . . Is she going to shop around for a new car?

9. plan . . . Are you going to start that novel over?

10. happen . . . While he was in Paris, did he come across the bakery I recommended?

Step 3: "No Hint" and Extra Comment

Listen to your teacher read part A **without** the extra verb and create part B yourself, remembering the verb from before. Add an extra comment to make your answer longer, and repeat until you can speak smoothly.

EXAMPLE:
plan . . . Are you going to start that novel over?
A) "plan . . . Are you going to start that novel over?"
B) "Yes, I plan to start it over. I started reading it a long time ago."

Step 4: Continue the Conversation!

Do Step 3 again but continue a short, back-and-forth conversation with your teacher or language partner.

EXAMPLE:
plan . . . Are you going to start that novel over?
A) "plan . . . Are you going to start that novel over?"
B) "Yes, I plan to start it over. I started reading it a long time ago."
A) "Is it a long novel?"
B) "It's pretty short, but I'm a slow reader."

Self-Study

Step 1: Read the examples aloud to get used to the pattern, and then go to Step 2.

Step 2: Read part A aloud and then try to create part B without looking at the text. Check your answers with the answer key. Repeat until you can speak part B smoothly without looking at the text.

Step 3: Cover the extra verbs with your hand or a sheet of paper. Read part A aloud **without** the extra verb and then create part B without looking at the text. Try to remember the verb from before. Add an extra comment to make your answer longer.

Step 4: Do step 3 again but continue a short, back-and-forth imaginary conversation. Practice while speaking aloud.

THE GOAL of this activity is to improve your small-talk skills by quickly asking a relevant question to keep the conversation going. Remember, being good at small talk means being good at asking questions! Use "it/them" and create a past or future tense question to match the situation.

Step 1: Shadowing

Listen to your teacher read parts A and B aloud, and repeat each sentence without looking at the text (the teacher may use the answer key). If you need to glance at the text, use part A (below).

Step 2: Independent Response

Next, listen to your teacher read part A (phrasal verb and sentence), and create part B yourself without looking at the text. Repeat until you can speak smoothly.

EXAMPLE

call back . . . My uncle left me a voicemail last week.
A) "call back . . . My uncle left me a voicemail last week."
B) "Did you call him back?"

A)

1. look after . . . They asked her to take care of their daughters next week.

2. come up with . . . He told me about a new way to improve my golf swing.

3. get over . . . I had horrible allergies last spring.

4. fill out . . . The employment agency gave her a dozen job applications.

5. try out . . . I just heard about a new social media app.

6. eat out . . . She doesn't want to cook at all this weekend.

7. call back . . . My uncle left me a voicemail last week.

8. shop around . . . They think their local electronics store is too expensive.

9. start over . . . She just started her speech, but her microphone isn't working.

10. come across . . . He was hoping to find his missing laptop.

Step 3: "No Hint"

Listen to your teacher read part A **without** the phrasal verb and create part B yourself, remembering the phrasal verb from context. Repeat until you can speak smoothly.

EXAMPLE:

call back . . . My uncle left me a voicemail last week.
A) "My uncle left me a voicemail last week."
B) "Did you call him back?"

Step 4: Continue the Conversation!

Do Step 3 again but continue a short, back-and-forth conversation with your teacher or language partner.

EXAMPLE:

call back . . . My uncle left me a voicemail last week.
A) "My uncle left me a voicemail last week."
B) "Did you call him back?"
A) "Yes, but I couldn't reach him."
B) "Are you close with your uncle?"
A) "We talk a few times a month, so we're pretty close."

Self-Study

Step 1: Read the examples aloud to get used to the pattern, and then go to Step 2.

Step 2: Read part A aloud and then try to create part B without looking at the text. Check your answers with the answer key. Repeat until you can speak part B smoothly without looking at the text.

Step 3: Cover the phrasal verbs with your hand or a sheet of paper. Read part A aloud **without** the phrasal verb and then create part B without looking at the text. Try to remember each phrasal verb from context. Repeat until you can speak smoothly and without hesitation.

Step 4: Do step 3 again but continue a short, back-and-forth imaginary conversation. Practice while speaking aloud.

CHAPTER

1. ask out

2. go back

3. drop by

4. hand out

5. hang around

6. close down

7. check on

8. bring over

9. look around

10. send back

5.1 QUICK CHANGES
Quickly change regular sentences into phrasal-verb sentences

THE GOAL of this activity is to learn the meaning of each phrasal verb through context. Change the original sentence into a new, more natural sentence using the phrasal verb. Try to keep the sentences as similar as possible and change the phrasal verb form if necessary.

Step 1: Shadowing

Listen to your teacher read parts A and B aloud, and repeat each sentence without looking at the text (the teacher may use the answer key). If you need to glance at the text, use part A (below).

Step 2: Independent Response

Next, listen to your teacher read part A (phrasal verb and sentence), and create part B yourself without looking at the text. Repeat until you can speak smoothly.

EXAMPLE

drop by . . . He usually goes to the convenience store after work.
A) "drop by . . . He usually goes to the convenience store after work."
B) "He usually drops by the convenience store after work."

A)

1. ask out . . . He often asks her to go out to dinner with him.

2. go back . . . She sometimes returns to the office at night.

3. drop by . . . He usually goes to the convenience store after work.

4. hand out . . . That store gives everyone free samples on weekends.

5. hang around . . . She likes to spend time at her friend's house on weeknights.

6. close down . . . I hope that little restaurant doesn't close permanently.

7. check on . . . She always takes a look at her sleeping baby at night to make sure he's ok.

8. bring over . . . Can you bring some sandwiches to my house?

9. look around . . . You should explore the new park.

10. send back . . . He returns a lot of Amazon orders through the mail.

11. check on . . . At work, I often need to confirm the status of our inventory.

Step 3: "No Hint" and Extra Comment

Listen to your teacher read part A **without** the phrasal verb and create part B yourself, remembering the phrasal verb from context. Add an extra comment to make your answer longer, and repeat until you can speak smoothly.

> **EXAMPLE:**
> drop by . . . He usually goes to the convenience store after work.
> A) "He usually goes to the convenience store after work."
> B) "He usually drops by the convenience store after work. He likes to buy snacks."

Step 4: Continue the Conversation!

Do Step 3 again but continue a short, back-and-forth conversation with your teacher or language partner.

> **EXAMPLE:**
> drop by . . . He usually goes to the convenience store after work.
> A) "He usually goes to the convenience store after work."
> B) "He usually drops by the convenience store after work. He likes to buy snacks."
> A) "What kind of snacks?"
> B) "He's trying to avoid sugar, so he buys salty snacks."

Self-Study

Step 1: Read the examples aloud to get used to the pattern, and then go to Step 2.

Step 2: Read part A aloud and then try to create part B without looking at the text. Check your answers with the answer key. Repeat until you can speak part B smoothly without looking at the text.

Step 3: Cover the phrasal verbs with your hand or a sheet of paper. Read part A aloud **without** the phrasal verb and then create part B without looking at the text. Try to remember each phrasal verb from context. Add an extra comment to make your answer longer.

Step 4: Do step 3 again but continue a short, back-and-forth imaginary conversation. Practice while speaking aloud.

THE GOAL of this activity is to give a quick, short answer using a phrasal verb in conversation. Use past tense and use "it/them" to keep your answer short and natural.

Step 1: Shadowing

Listen to your teacher read parts A and B aloud, and repeat each sentence without looking at the text (the teacher may use the answer key). If you need to glance at the text, use part A (below).

Step 2: Independent Response

Next, listen to your teacher read part A (phrasal verb and sentence), and create part B yourself without looking at the text. Repeat until you can speak smoothly.

EXAMPLE

hand out . . . Did you distribute nametags to everyone?
A) "hand out . . . Did you distribute nametags to everyone?"
B) "I handed them out."

A)

1. ask out . . . Did she ask her coworkers to go out for drinks with her?

2. go back . . . Did he return to the station to look for his iPhone?

3. drop by . . . Did they visit your house for a short time?

4. hand out . . . Did you distribute nametags to everyone?

5. hang around . . . Did he spend some extra time at the casino?

6. close down . . . Did that company stop doing business?

7. check on . . . Did you check to see what the kids were doing?

8. bring over . . . Did she bring her laptop to your house?

9. look around . . . Did he explore Taipei on his business trip?

10. send back . . . Did they return the clothes they ordered online?

Step 3: "No Hint" and Extra Comment

Listen to your teacher read part A **without** the phrasal verb and create part B yourself, remembering the phrasal verb from context. Add an extra comment to make your answer longer, and repeat until you can speak smoothly.

EXAMPLE:

hand out . . . Did you distribute nametags to everyone?

A) "Did you distribute nametags to everyone?"

B) "I handed them out. This is a big conference, so I'm glad we all have nametags."

Step 4: Continue the Conversation!

Do Step 3 again but continue a short, back-and-forth conversation with your teacher or language partner.

EXAMPLE:

hand out . . . Did you distribute nametags to everyone?

A) "Did you distribute nametags to everyone?"

B) "I handed them out. This is a big conference, so I'm glad we all have nametags."

A) "Are there more people here than you expected?"

B) "Yes, I thought more people would choose the online option."

Self-Study

Step 1: Read the examples aloud to get used to the pattern, and then go to Step 2.

Step 2: Read part A aloud and then try to create part B without looking at the text. Check your answers with the answer key. Repeat until you can speak part B smoothly without looking at the text.

Step 3: Cover the phrasal verbs with your hand or a sheet of paper. Read part A aloud **without** the phrasal verb and then create part B without looking at the text. Try to remember each phrasal verb from context. Add an extra comment to make your answer longer.

Step 4: Do step 3 again but continue a short, back-and-forth imaginary conversation. Practice while speaking aloud.

5.3 QUICK BUILDER
Quickly build more detailed answers

THE GOAL of this activity is to add more detail to your answer quickly with an extra verb. Follow the pattern (verb + to + phrasal verb) and create a past or future tense answer. Use "it/them" for a short, natural response.

Step 1: Shadowing

Listen to your teacher read parts A and B aloud, and repeat each sentence without looking at the text (the teacher may use the answer key). If you need to glance at the text, use part A (below).

Step 2: Independent Response

Next, listen to your teacher read part A (extra verb and sentence), and create part B yourself without looking at the text. Repeat until you can speak smoothly.

EXAMPLE

decide not . . . Did they hand out free bottled water at the race?
A) "decide not . . . Did they hand out free bottled water at the race?"
B) "They decided not to hand it out."

A)

1. plan . . . Are you going to ask them out to that Indian restaurant?

2. agree . . . Did he go back to his parents' house last weekend?

3. hope . . . Are you going to drop by the football game later?

4. decide not . . . Did they hand out free bottled water at the race?

5. want . . . Did his daughter hang around the mall with her friends last night?

6. appear . . . Did that electronics store close down for a while last year?

7. promise . . . Is he going to check on the turkey in the oven?

8. forget . . . Did she bring over her homework?

9. decide . . . Did the police look around the crime scene?

10. remember . . . Did you send back the book you borrowed from your cousin?

Step 3: "No Hint" and Extra Comment

Listen to your teacher read part A **without** the extra verb and create part B yourself, remembering the verb from before. Add an extra comment to make your answer longer, and repeat until you can speak smoothly.

EXAMPLE:

decide not . . . Did they hand out free bottled water at the race?
A) "Did they hand out free bottled water at the race?"
B) "They decided not to hand it out. The runners had to bring water or buy it."

Step 4: Continue the Conversation!

Do Step 3 again but continue a short, back-and-forth conversation with your teacher or language partner.

EXAMPLE:

decide not . . . Did they hand out free bottled water at the race?
A) "Did they hand out free bottled water at the race?"
B) "They decided not to hand it out. The runners had to bring water or buy it."
A) "That's too bad."
B) "Well, it was a charity event, so they were trying to raise money."

Self-Study

Step 1: Read the examples aloud to get used to the pattern, and then go to Step 2.

Step 2: Read part A aloud and then try to create part B without looking at the text. Check your answers with the answer key. Repeat until you can speak part B smoothly without looking at the text.

Step 3: Cover the extra verbs with your hand or a sheet of paper. Read part A aloud **without** the extra verb and then create part B without looking at the text. Try to remember the verb from before. Add an extra comment to make your answer longer.

Step 4: Do step 3 again but continue a short, back-and-forth imaginary conversation. Practice while speaking aloud.

QUICK QUESTIONS
Quickly ask questions to keep the conversation going

THE GOAL of this activity is to improve your small-talk skills by quickly asking a relevant question to keep the conversation going. Remember, being good at small talk means being good at asking questions! Use "it/them" and create a past or future tense question to match the situation.

Step 1: Shadowing

Listen to your teacher read parts A and B aloud, and repeat each sentence without looking at the text (the teacher may use the answer key). If you need to glance at the text, use part A (below).

Step 2: Independent Response

Next, listen to your teacher read part A (phrasal verb and sentence), and create part B yourself without looking at the text. Repeat until you can speak smoothly.

EXAMPLE

close down . . . My favorite farmers market is struggling to make money.
A) "close down . . . My favorite farmers market is struggling to make money."
B) "Is it going to close down?"

A)

1. ask out . . . She wants to go to the school dance with him.

2. go back . . . He planned to return to San Francisco last year.

3. drop by . . . They told me they would stop at my house on their way to Chicago.

4. hand out . . . She has a lot of flyers to advertise her new business.

5. hang around . . . We invited my son's friends to stay and play games after dinner.

6. close down . . . My favorite farmers market is struggling to make money.

7. check on . . . His dog was barking a lot in the backyard.

8. bring over . . . I'm sick, and my neighbor just called to say she's making dinner for me.

9. look around . . . I couldn't find a good cafe near my hotel.

10. send back . . . Her new smart TV was just delivered, but it doesn't work.

Step 3: "No Hint"

Listen to your teacher read part A **without** the phrasal verb and create part B yourself, remembering the phrasal verb from context. Repeat until you can speak smoothly.

EXAMPLE:

close down . . . My favorite farmers market is struggling to make money.
A) "My favorite farmers market is struggling to make money."
B) "Is it going to close down?"

Step 4: Continue the Conversation!

Do Step 3 again but continue a short, back-and-forth conversation with your teacher or language partner.

EXAMPLE:

close down . . . My favorite farmers market is struggling to make money.
A) "My favorite farmers market is struggling to make money."
B) "Is it going to close down?"
A) "I don't know, but there are fewer and fewer farmers there every year."
B) "What do you usually buy there?"
A) "I buy most of my vegetables there, and apples in fall."

Self-Study

Step 1: Read the examples aloud to get used to the pattern, and then go to Step 2.

Step 2: Read part A aloud and then try to create part B without looking at the text. Check your answers with the answer key. Repeat until you can speak part B smoothly without looking at the text.

Step 3: Cover the phrasal verbs with your hand or a sheet of paper. Read part A aloud **without** the phrasal verb and then create part B without looking at the text. Try to remember each phrasal verb from context. Repeat until you can speak smoothly and without hesitation.

Step 4: Do step 3 again but continue a short, back-and-forth imaginary conversation. Practice while speaking aloud.

CHAPTER

1. meet with

2. have over

3. get back

4. go down

5. send out

6. let in(to)

7. help out

8. shut off

9. look up

10. check into

6.1 QUICK CHANGES
Quickly change regular sentences into phrasal-verb sentences

THE GOAL of this activity is to learn the meaning of each phrasal verb through context. Change the original sentence into a new, more natural sentence using the phrasal verb. Try to keep the sentences as similar as possible and change the phrasal verb form if necessary.

Step 1: Shadowing

Listen to your teacher read parts A and B aloud, and repeat each sentence without looking at the text (the teacher may use the answer key). If you need to glance at the text, use part A (below).

Step 2: Independent Response

Next, listen to your teacher read part A (phrasal verb and sentence), and create part B yourself without looking at the text. Repeat until you can speak smoothly.

EXAMPLE
look up . . . I usually search for directions on my phone.
A) "look up . . . I usually search for directions on my phone."
B) "I usually look up directions on my phone."

A)

1. meet with . . . She often has a meeting with her boss on Fridays.

2. have over . . . I have my parents come to my house every Sunday.

3. get back . . . He returns home from work by 6 p.m.

4. go down . . . I hope the price of gas decreases.

5. send out . . . They always mail New Year's cards to all their friends.

6. let into . . . It's a little early, but I hope they let us enter the cafe.

7. help out . . . She helps her team members at work.

8. shut off . . . Can you turn off the sink?

9. look up . . . I usually search for directions on my phone.

10. check into . . . I want to get more information about piano lessons for my son.

11. get back . . . Did she retrieve her lost purse?

12. let into . . . I love playing guitar, so I hope they allow me to join their band.

Step 3: "No Hint" and Extra Comment

Listen to your teacher read part A **without** the phrasal verb and create part B yourself, remembering the phrasal verb from context. Add an extra comment to make your answer longer, and repeat until you can speak smoothly.

EXAMPLE:
look up . . . I usually search for directions on my phone.
A) "I usually search for directions on my phone."
B) "I usually look up directions on my phone. I have a bad sense of direction."

Step 4: Continue the Conversation!

Do Step 3 again but continue a short, back-and-forth conversation with your teacher or language partner.

EXAMPLE:
look up . . . I usually search for directions on my phone.
A) "I usually search for directions on my phone."
B) "I usually look up directions on my phone. I have a bad sense of direction."
A) "What app do you use?"
B) "I prefer Google Maps, even on my iPhone."

Self-Study

Step 1: Read the examples aloud to get used to the pattern, and then go to Step 2.

Step 2: Read part A aloud and then try to create part B without looking at the text. Check your answers with the answer key. Repeat until you can speak part B smoothly without looking at the text.

Step 3: Cover the phrasal verbs with your hand or a sheet of paper. Read part A aloud **without** the phrasal verb and then create part B without looking at the text. Try to remember each phrasal verb from context. Add an extra comment to make your answer longer.

Step 4: Do step 3 again but continue a short, back-and-forth imaginary conversation. Practice while speaking aloud.

6.2 QUICK ANSWERS
Answer questions quickly and naturally

THE GOAL of this activity is to give a quick, short answer using a phrasal verb in conversation. Use past tense and use "it/them" to keep your answer short and natural.

Step 1: Shadowing
Listen to your teacher read parts A and B aloud, and repeat each sentence without looking at the text (the teacher may use the answer key). If you need to glance at the text, use part A (below).

Step 2: Independent Response
Next, listen to your teacher read part A (phrasal verb and sentence), and create part B yourself without looking at the text. Repeat until you can speak smoothly.

EXAMPLE
send out . . . Did you send the new schedule in that group email?
A) "send out . . . Did you send the new schedule in that group email?"
B) "I sent it out."

A)

1. meet with . . . Did you get together with your Dutch clients?

2. have over . . . Did he invite his in-laws to his house?

3. get back . . . Did she retrieve her lost iPhone?

4. go down . . . Did the temperature drop last night?

5. send out . . . Did you send the new schedule in that group email?

6. let in . . . Did they allow him to join their football club?

7. help out . . . Did the shop staff assist you?

8. shut off . . . Did she turn off the gas heater?

9. look up . . . Did you check those English words in the dictionary?

10. check into . . . Did he find more information about renting a car?

Step 3: "No Hint" and Extra Comment

Listen to your teacher read part A **without** the phrasal verb and create part B yourself, remembering the phrasal verb from context. Add an extra comment to make your answer longer, and repeat until you can speak smoothly.

EXAMPLE:

send out . . . Did you send the new schedule in that group email?
A) "Did you send the new schedule in that group email?"
B) "I sent it out. I hope all my team members actually read that email."

Step 4: Continue the Conversation!

Do Step 3 again but continue a short, back-and-forth conversation with your teacher or language partner.

EXAMPLE:

send out . . . Did you send the new schedule in that group email?
A) "Did you send the new schedule in that group email?"
B) "I sent it out. I hope all my team members actually read that email."
A) "Do they usually ignore your emails?"
B) "No, but we get so many emails every day, we often miss the important ones!"

Self-Study

Step 1: Read the examples aloud to get used to the pattern, and then go to Step 2.

Step 2: Read part A aloud and then try to create part B without looking at the text. Check your answers with the answer key. Repeat until you can speak part B smoothly without looking at the text.

Step 3: Cover the phrasal verbs with your hand or a sheet of paper. Read part A aloud **without** the phrasal verb and then create part B without looking at the text. Try to remember each phrasal verb from context. Add an extra comment to make your answer longer.

Step 4: Do step 3 again but continue a short, back-and-forth imaginary conversation. Practice while speaking aloud.

QUICK BUILDER
Quickly build more detailed answers

THE GOAL of this activity is to add more detail to your answer quickly with an extra verb. Follow the pattern (verb + to + phrasal verb) and create a past or future tense answer. Use "it/them" for a short, natural response.

Step 1: Shadowing
Listen to your teacher read parts A and B aloud, and repeat each sentence without looking at the text (the teacher may use the answer key). If you need to glance at the text, use part A (below).

Step 2: Independent Response
Next, listen to your teacher read part A (extra verb and sentence), and create part B yourself without looking at the text. Repeat until you can speak smoothly.

EXAMPLE
decide not . . . Did you meet with your professor last week?
A) "decide not . . . Did you meet with your professor last week?"
B) "I decided not to meet with her."

A)

1. decide not . . . Did you meet with your professor last week?

2. plan . . . Is he going to have his photography club over?

3. try . . . Did you get your money back from that email scam?

4. seem . . . Did your son's fever go down today?

5. remember . . . Did she send out those invitations?

6. agree . . . Are they going to let customers into the gym before 6:00 a.m.?

7. promise . . . Is she going to help out her nephew by donating to his fundraiser?

8. forget . . . Did you shut off the TV?

9. plan . . . Is he going to look up the instructions for that Ikea table?

10. decide . . . Did you check into that new budget airline?

Step 3: "No Hint" and Extra Comment

Listen to your teacher read part A **without** the extra verb and create part B yourself, remembering the verb from before. Add an extra comment to make your answer longer, and repeat until you can speak smoothly.

EXAMPLE:

decide not . . . Did you meet with your professor last week?
A) "Did you meet with your professor last week?"
B) "I decided not to meet with her. I need to finish my project first."

Step 4: Continue the Conversation!

Do Step 3 again but continue a short, back-and-forth conversation with your teacher or language partner.

EXAMPLE:

decide not . . . Did you meet with your professor last week?
A) "Did you meet with your professor last week?"
B) "I decided not to meet with her. I need to finish my project first."
A) "When is your deadline?"
B) "This weekend, and I hope I can finish it on time!"

Self-Study

Step 1: Read the examples aloud to get used to the pattern, and then go to Step 2.

Step 2: Read part A aloud and then try to create part B without looking at the text. Check your answers with the answer key. Repeat until you can speak part B smoothly without looking at the text.

Step 3: Cover the extra verbs with your hand or a sheet of paper. Read part A aloud **without** the extra verb and then create part B without looking at the text. Try to remember the verb from before. Add an extra comment to make your answer longer.

Step 4: Do step 3 again but continue a short, back-and-forth imaginary conversation. Practice while speaking aloud.

THE GOAL of this activity is to improve your small-talk skills by quickly asking a relevant question to keep the conversation going. Remember, being good at small talk means being good at asking questions! Use "it/them" and create a past or future tense question to match the situation.

Step 1: Shadowing

Listen to your teacher read parts A and B aloud, and repeat each sentence without looking at the text (the teacher may use the answer key). If you need to glance at the text, use part A (below).

Step 2: Independent Response

Next, listen to your teacher read part A (phrasal verb and sentence), and create part B yourself without looking at the text. Repeat until you can speak smoothly.

EXAMPLE

check into . . . She heard that she was eligible for a promotion.
A) "check into . . . She heard that she was eligible for a promotion."
B) "Did she check into it?"

A)

1. meet with . . . He considered scheduling an appointment with his therapist last week.

2. have over . . . They want to have a barbecue party with their neighbors.

3. get back . . . My dry cleaner said he couldn't find my winter coat.

4. go down . . . I was hoping that house prices would decrease in Florida last year.

5. send out . . . The company asked her to mail them a hard copy of her resume.

6. let in . . . My dog is really muddy, but he wants to come into the house.

7. help out . . . Her brother asked her for financial help last year.

8. shut off . . . My neighbor's car alarm was going off early this morning.

9. look up . . . He plans to cook paella, but he doesn't know how!

10. check into . . . She heard that she was eligible for a promotion.

Step 3: "No Hint"

Listen to your teacher read part A **without** the phrasal verb and create part B yourself, remembering the phrasal verb from context. Repeat until you can speak smoothly.

EXAMPLE:

check into . . . She heard that she was eligible for a promotion.
A) "She heard that she was eligible for a promotion."
B) "Did she check into it?"

Step 4: Continue the Conversation!

Do Step 3 again but continue a short, back-and-forth conversation with your teacher or language partner.

EXAMPLE:

check into . . . She heard that she was eligible for a promotion.
A) "She heard that she was eligible for a promotion."
B) "Did she check into it?"
A) "Yes, even though she was nervous to ask her boss about it."
B) "What happened?"
A) "She got promoted!"

Self-Study

Step 1: Read the examples aloud to get used to the pattern, and then go to Step 2.

Step 2: Read part A aloud and then try to create part B without looking at the text. Check your answers with the answer key. Repeat until you can speak part B smoothly without looking at the text.

Step 3: Cover the phrasal verbs with your hand or a sheet of paper. Read part A aloud **without** the phrasal verb and then create part B without looking at the text. Try to remember each phrasal verb from context. Repeat until you can speak smoothly and without hesitation.

Step 4: Do step 3 again but continue a short, back-and-forth imaginary conversation. Practice while speaking aloud.

CHAPTER 7

1. take off

2. hand in

3. go out

4. warm up

5. take back

6. look forward to

7. set up

8. drop off

9. wake up

10. turn down

QUICK CHANGES
Quickly change regular sentences into phrasal-verb sentences

THE GOAL of this activity is to learn the meaning of each phrasal verb through context. Change the original sentence into a new, more natural sentence using the phrasal verb. Try to keep the sentences as similar as possible and change the phrasal verb form if necessary.

Step 1: Shadowing

Listen to your teacher read parts A and B aloud, and repeat each sentence without looking at the text (the teacher may use the answer key). If you need to glance at the text, use part A (below).

Step 2: Independent Response

Next, listen to your teacher read part A (phrasal verb and sentence), and create part B yourself without looking at the text. Repeat until you can speak smoothly.

EXAMPLE

drop off (at) . . . I take my kids to school every morning.
A) "drop off at . . . I take my kids to school every morning."
B) "I drop off my kids at school every morning."

A)

1. take off . . . I can't take vacation time from work in December.

2. hand in . . . Did you submit your essay to the professor?

3. go out . . . They always go to the bars on weekends.

4. warm up . . . On cold days, you should heat your car before driving.

5. take back . . . He often returns clothes to the store.

6. look forward to . . . She always gets excited about her business trips.

7. set up . . . They love camping, and they can quickly construct their tent.

8. drop off (at) . . . I take my kids to school every morning.

9. wake up . . . He usually awakens at 6:00 a.m.

10. turn down . . . She loves her company, so she always refuses other job offers.

11. take off . . . It's hot in here, so I need to remove my wool sweater.

12. set up . . . She decided to arrange an online meeting with all of her colleagues.

13. turn down . . . I'm cold, so could you reduce the power of the air conditioning?

Step 3: "No Hint" and Extra Comment

Listen to your teacher read part A **without** the phrasal verb and create part B yourself, remembering the phrasal verb from context. Add an extra comment to make your answer longer, and repeat until you can speak smoothly.

EXAMPLE:

drop off (at) . . . I take my kids to school every morning.
A) "I take my kids to school every morning."
B) "I drop off my kids at school every morning. I don't want them to walk to school."

Step 4: Continue the Conversation!

Do Step 3 again but continue a short, back-and-forth conversation with your teacher or language partner.

EXAMPLE:

drop off (at) . . . I take my kids to school every morning.
A) "I take my kids to school every morning."
B) "I drop off my kids at school every morning. I don't want them to walk to school."
A) "Do you live in a dangerous area?"
B) "Not really, but my kids are very young."

Self-Study

Step 1: Read the examples aloud to get used to the pattern, and then go to Step 2.

Step 2: Read part A aloud and then try to create part B without looking at the text. Check your answers with the answer key. Repeat until you can speak part B smoothly without looking at the text.

Step 3: Cover the phrasal verbs with your hand or a sheet of paper. Read part A aloud **without** the phrasal verb and then create part B without looking at the text. Try to remember each phrasal verb from context. Add an extra comment to make your answer longer.

Step 4: Do step 3 again but continue a short, back-and-forth imaginary conversation. Practice while speaking aloud.

THE GOAL of this activity is to give a quick, short answer using a phrasal verb in conversation. Use past tense and use "it/them" to keep your answer short and natural.

Step 1: Shadowing

Listen to your teacher read parts A and B aloud, and repeat each sentence without looking at the text (the teacher may use the answer key). If you need to glance at the text, use part A (below).

Step 2: Independent Response

Next, listen to your teacher read part A (phrasal verb and sentence), and create part B yourself without looking at the text. Repeat until you can speak smoothly.

EXAMPLE

set up . . . Did you organize that meet-and-greet event?
A) "set up . . . Did you organize that meet-and-greet event?"
B) "I set it up."

A)

1. take off . . . Did you remove your shoes before entering the house?

2. hand in . . . Did he give his two weeks' notice to his manager?

3. go out . . . Did they go on a date last night?

4. warm up . . . Did she finally get warm after walking in the snowstorm?

5. take back . . . Did he return that broken laptop to the store?

6. look forward to . . . Did you expect to have fun at the party?

7. set up . . . Did you organize that meet-and-greet event?

8. drop off . . . Did you deliver those books to your friend's house?

9. wake up . . . Did she finally awaken the kids?

10. turn down . . . Did he lower the TV volume?

Step 3: "No Hint" and Extra Comment

Listen to your teacher read part A **without** the phrasal verb and create part B yourself, remembering the phrasal verb from context. Add an extra comment to make your answer longer, and repeat until you can speak smoothly.

EXAMPLE:
set up . . . Did you organize that meet-and-greet event?
A) "Did you organize that meet-and-greet event?"
B) "I set it up. I booked a conference room at the Hilton Hotel."

Step 4: Continue the Conversation!

Do Step 3 again but continue a short, back-and-forth conversation with your teacher or language partner.

EXAMPLE:
set up . . . Did you organize that meet-and-greet event?
A) "Did you organize that meet-and-greet event?"
B) "I set it up. I booked a conference room at the Hilton Hotel."
A) "That sounds expensive!"
B) "Well, we need to impress our new clients."

Self-Study

Step 1: Read the examples aloud to get used to the pattern, and then go to Step 2.

Step 2: Read part A aloud and then try to create part B without looking at the text. Check your answers with the answer key. Repeat until you can speak part B smoothly without looking at the text.

Step 3: Cover the phrasal verbs with your hand or a sheet of paper. Read part A aloud **without** the phrasal verb and then create part B without looking at the text. Try to remember each phrasal verb from context. Add an extra comment to make your answer longer.

Step 4: Do step 3 again but continue a short, back-and-forth imaginary conversation. Practice while speaking aloud.

THE GOAL of this activity is to add more detail to your answer quickly with an extra verb. Follow the pattern (verb + to + phrasal verb) and create a past or future tense answer. Use "it/them" for a short, natural response.

Step 1: Shadowing

Listen to your teacher read parts A and B aloud, and repeat each sentence without looking at the text (the teacher may use the answer key). If you need to glance at the text, use part A (below).

Step 2: Independent Response

Next, listen to your teacher read part A (extra verb and sentence), and create part B yourself without looking at the text. Repeat until you can speak smoothly.

EXAMPLE

try . . . Did you look forward to retirement?
A) "try . . . Did you look forward to retirement?"
B) "I tried to look forward to it."

A)

1. plan . . . Is she going to take next Tuesday off?

2. remember . . . Did he hand in his English homework?

3. want . . . Are they going to go out for drinks tonight?

4. forget . . . Did you warm up before the race?

5. decide not . . . Are you going to take back those damaged headphones?

6. try . . . Did you look forward to retirement?

7. promise . . . Is he going to set up more tables in the conference room?

8. agree . . . Did she drop off the paperwork at the bank?

9. try . . . Did you wake up early this morning?

10. decide . . . Did he turn down that free flight?

Step 3: "No Hint" and Extra Comment

Listen to your teacher read part A **without** the extra verb and create part B yourself, remembering the verb from before. Add an extra comment to make your answer longer, and repeat until you can speak smoothly.

EXAMPLE:

try . . . Did you look forward to retirement?
A) "Did you look forward to retirement?"
B) "I tried to look forward to it. I was worried I might get bored without a job."

Step 4: Continue the Conversation!

Do Step 3 again but continue a short, back-and-forth conversation with your teacher or language partner.

EXAMPLE:

try . . . Did you look forward to retirement?
A) "Did you look forward to retirement?"
B) "I tried to look forward to it. I was worried I might get bored without a job."
A) "Well, how is it going? Is life dull now that you've retired?"
B) "Not at all! I've started coaching high school football, and it keeps me very busy."

Self-Study

Step 1: Read the examples aloud to get used to the pattern, and then go to Step 2.

Step 2: Read part A aloud and then try to create part B without looking at the text. Check your answers with the answer key. Repeat until you can speak part B smoothly without looking at the text.

Step 3: Cover the extra verbs with your hand or a sheet of paper. Read part A aloud **without** the extra verb and then create part B without looking at the text. Try to remember the verb from before. Add an extra comment to make your answer longer.

Step 4: Do step 3 again but continue a short, back-and-forth imaginary conversation. Practice while speaking aloud.

THE GOAL of this activity is to improve your small-talk skills by quickly asking a relevant question to keep the conversation going. Remember, being good at small talk means being good at asking questions! Use "it/them" and create a past or future tense question to match the situation.

Step 1: Shadowing

Listen to your teacher read parts A and B aloud, and repeat each sentence without looking at the text (the teacher may use the answer key). If you need to glance at the text, use part A (below).

Step 2: Independent Response

Next, listen to your teacher read part A (phrasal verb and sentence), and create part B yourself without looking at the text. Repeat until you can speak smoothly.

EXAMPLE

look forward to . . . She seemed excited about her presentation last week.
A) "look forward to . . . She seemed excited about her presentation last week."
B) "Did she look forward to it?" / "Was she looking forward to it?"

A)

1. take off . . . They asked him to remove his baseball cap when he entered the church.

2. hand in . . . She just finished writing her history essay, but it's too short.

3. go out . . . My coworkers wanted to go to the bars last night.

4. warm up . . . The kids were really cold after ice skating.

5. take back . . . My new shoes are very uncomfortable.

6. look forward to . . . She seemed excited about her presentation last week.

7. set up . . . They have some great ideas for our new company website.

8. drop off . . . He bought a birthday present for his grandmother.

9. wake up . . . I set my alarm for 3:00 a.m. yesterday.

10. turn down . . . They have a wedding invitation, but they don't want to travel in winter.

Step 3: "No Hint"

Listen to your teacher read part A **without** the phrasal verb and create part B yourself, remembering the phrasal verb from context. Repeat until you can speak smoothly.

EXAMPLE:

look forward to . . . She seemed excited about her presentation last week.
A) "She seemed excited about her presentation last week."
B) "Did she look forward to it?" / "Was she looking forward to it?"

Step 4: Continue the Conversation!

Do Step 3 again but continue a short, back-and-forth conversation with your teacher or language partner.

EXAMPLE:

look forward to . . . She seemed excited about her presentation last week.
A) "She seemed excited about her presentation last week."
B) "Did she look forward to it?" / "Was she looking forward to it?"
A) "Yes. She's outgoing and she enjoys public speaking."
B) "How many people attended?"
A) "Her whole department was there. They always enjoy her presentations."

Self-Study

Step 1: Read the examples aloud to get used to the pattern, and then go to Step 2.

Step 2: Read part A aloud and then try to create part B without looking at the text. Check your answers with the answer key. Repeat until you can speak part B smoothly without looking at the text.

Step 3: Cover the phrasal verbs with your hand or a sheet of paper. Read part A aloud **without** the phrasal verb and then create part B without looking at the text. Try to remember each phrasal verb from context. Repeat until you can speak smoothly and without hesitation.

Step 4: Do step 3 again but continue a short, back-and-forth imaginary conversation. Practice while speaking aloud.

CHAPTER

1. cool off

2. leave behind

3. mess up

4. put up

5. come over

6. sign up

7. take out

8. cheer up

9. go away

10. line up

THE GOAL of this activity is to learn the meaning of each phrasal verb through context. Change the original sentence into a new, more natural sentence using the phrasal verb. Try to keep the sentences as similar as possible and change the phrasal verb form if necessary.

Step 1: Shadowing

Listen to your teacher read parts A and B aloud, and repeat each sentence without looking at the text (the teacher may use the answer key). If you need to glance at the text, use part A (below).

Step 2: Independent Response

Next, listen to your teacher read part A (phrasal verb and sentence), and create part B yourself without looking at the text. Repeat until you can speak smoothly.

EXAMPLE

line up . . . Customers always stand in line outside that restaurant.
A) "line up . . . Customers always stand in line outside that restaurant."
B) "Customers always line up outside that restaurant."

A)

1. cool off . . . In summer, it's nice to get cool in the swimming pool.

2. leave behind . . . He leaves his family in Japan when he's working abroad.

3. mess up . . . She doesn't often make mistakes on tests.

4. put up . . . I place decorations in my house every December.

5. come over . . . My friends usually come to my house on weekends.

6. sign up . . . You should register for that online course.

7. take out . . . She always asks him to carry the garbage outside.

8. cheer up . . . It's easy to feel happier when the sun is shining.

9. go away . . . I hope my neighbor's big dog leaves before I go outside.

10. line up . . . Customers always stand in line outside that restaurant.

11. leave behind . . . She always forgets her sunglasses when she goes on a trip.

12. mess up . . . Tell the kids not to make a mess of the house while I'm gone.

13. take out . . . He takes his daughter to a restaurant for dinner once a week.

14. line up . . . I need to arrange a lot of meetings this week.

Step 3: "No Hint" and Extra Comment

Listen to your teacher read part A **without** the phrasal verb and create part B yourself, remembering the phrasal verb from context. Add an extra comment to make your answer longer, and repeat until you can speak smoothly.

EXAMPLE:
line up . . . Customers always stand in line outside that restaurant.
A) "Customers always stand in line outside that restaurant."
B) "Customers always line up outside that restaurant. The food is great there!"

Step 4: Continue the Conversation!

Do Step 3 again but continue a short, back-and-forth conversation with your teacher or language partner.

EXAMPLE:
line up . . . Customers always stand in line outside that restaurant.
A) "Customers always stand in line outside that restaurant."
B) "Customers always line up outside that restaurant. The food is great there!"
A) "How often do you go there?"
B) "About once a week. It's not too expensive, and they change the menu often."

Self-Study

Step 1: Read the examples aloud to get used to the pattern, and then go to Step 2.

Step 2: Read part A aloud and then try to create part B without looking at the text. Check your answers with the answer key. Repeat until you can speak part B smoothly without looking at the text.

Step 3: Cover the phrasal verbs with your hand or a sheet of paper. Read part A aloud **without** the phrasal verb and then create part B without looking at the text. Try to remember each phrasal verb from context. Add an extra comment to make your answer longer.

Step 4: Do step 3 again but continue a short, back-and-forth imaginary conversation. Practice while speaking aloud.

8.2 QUICK ANSWERS
Answer questions quickly and naturally

THE GOAL of this activity is to give a quick, short answer using a phrasal verb in conversation. Use past tense and use "it/them" to keep your answer short and natural.

Step 1: Shadowing
Listen to your teacher read parts A and B aloud, and repeat each sentence without looking at the text (the teacher may use the answer key). If you need to glance at the text, use part A (below).

Step 2: Independent Response
Next, listen to your teacher read part A (phrasal verb and sentence), and create part B yourself without looking at the text. Repeat until you can speak smoothly.

EXAMPLE
come over . . . Did he arrive at your house yesterday?
A) "come over . . . Did he arrive at your house yesterday?"
B) "He came over."

A)

1. cool off . . . Did the weather get cooler yesterday?

2. leave behind . . . Did you leave your down jacket at home?

3. mess up . . . Did the kids make a mess of the flower arrangement?

4. put up . . . Did she display her painting on the wall?

5. come over . . . Did he arrive at your house yesterday?

6. sign up . . . Did you register for those free classes?

7. take out . . . Did she take them to a restaurant for dinner?

8. cheer up . . . Did they make her feel better?

9. go away . . . Did the mosquitoes disappear last week?

10. line up . . . Did you arrange your job interviews for next week?

Step 3: "No Hint" and Extra Comment

Listen to your teacher read part A **without** the phrasal verb and create part B yourself, remembering the phrasal verb from context. Add an extra comment to make your answer longer, and repeat until you can speak smoothly.

EXAMPLE:
come over . . . Did he arrive at your house yesterday?
A) "Did he arrive at your house yesterday?"
B) "He came over. It was almost 11:00 p.m."

Step 4: Continue the Conversation!

Do Step 3 again but continue a short, back-and-forth conversation with your teacher or language partner.

EXAMPLE:
come over . . . Did he arrive at your house yesterday?
A) "Did he arrive at your house yesterday?"
B) "He came over. It was almost 11:00 p.m."
A) "Why did he come over so late?"
B) "We wanted to go to that new movie together, and it was a midnight showing."

Self-Study

Step 1: Read the examples aloud to get used to the pattern, and then go to Step 2.

Step 2: Read part A aloud and then try to create part B without looking at the text. Check your answers with the answer key. Repeat until you can speak part B smoothly without looking at the text.

Step 3: Cover the phrasal verbs with your hand or a sheet of paper. Read part A aloud **without** the phrasal verb and then create part B without looking at the text. Try to remember each phrasal verb from context. Add an extra comment to make your answer longer.

Step 4: Do step 3 again but continue a short, back-and-forth imaginary conversation. Practice while speaking aloud.

QUICK BUILDER
Quickly build more detailed answers

THE GOAL of this activity is to add more detail to your answer quickly with an extra verb. Follow the pattern (verb + to + phrasal verb) and create a past or future tense answer. Use "it/them" for a short, natural response.

Step 1: Shadowing
Listen to your teacher read parts A and B aloud, and repeat each sentence without looking at the text (the teacher may use the answer key). If you need to glance at the text, use part A (below).

Step 2: Independent Response
Next, listen to your teacher read part A (extra verb and sentence), and create part B yourself without looking at the text. Repeat until you can speak smoothly.

EXAMPLE
try . . . Did you cool off your dog in the shade at the park?
A) "try . . . Did you cool off your dog in the shade at the park?"
B) "I tried to cool him off."

A)

1. try . . . Did you cool off your dog in the shade at the park?

2. promise . . . Is she going to leave her car behind for her daughter to use?

3. try not . . . Did she mess up her dress before the wedding?

4. decide . . . Are you going to put up those new family photos?

5. forget . . . Did he come over last Saturday?

6. plan . . . Is he going to sign up for those company English classes?

7. remember . . . Did they take the extra tables out of the conference room?

8. try . . . Did she cheer up her kids last weekend when it was raining?

9. seem . . . Did the humidity go away last week?

10. decide not . . . Did the teacher line up her students for the fire drill?

Step 3: "No Hint" and Extra Comment

Listen to your teacher read part A **without** the extra verb and create part B yourself, remembering the verb from before. Add an extra comment to make your answer longer, and repeat until you can speak smoothly.

EXAMPLE:
try . . . Did you cool off your dog in the shade at the park?
A) "Did you cool off your dog in the shade at the park?"
B) "I tried to cool him off. He was really hot, and he drank a lot of water."

Step 4: Continue the Conversation!

Do Step 3 again but continue a short, back-and-forth conversation with your teacher or language partner.

EXAMPLE:
try . . . Did you cool off your dog in the shade at the park?
A) "Did you cool off your dog in the shade?"
B) "I tried to cool him off. He was really hot, and he drank a lot of water."
A) "Do you usually bring a water bowl with you?"
B) "Because it's so humid these days, I always bring a water bowl in my backpack."

Self-Study

Step 1: Read the examples aloud to get used to the pattern, and then go to Step 2.

Step 2: Read part A aloud and then try to create part B without looking at the text. Check your answers with the answer key. Repeat until you can speak part B smoothly without looking at the text.

Step 3: Cover the extra verbs with your hand or a sheet of paper. Read part A aloud **without** the extra verb and then create part B without looking at the text. Try to remember the verb from before. Add an extra comment to make your answer longer.

Step 4: Do step 3 again but continue a short, back-and-forth imaginary conversation. Practice while speaking aloud.

THE GOAL of this activity is to improve your small-talk skills by quickly asking a relevant question to keep the conversation going. Remember, being good at small talk means being good at asking questions! Use "it/them" and create a past or future tense question to match the situation.

Step 1: Shadowing

Listen to your teacher read parts A and B aloud, and repeat each sentence without looking at the text (the teacher may use the answer key). If you need to glance at the text, use part A (below).

Step 2: Independent Response

Next, listen to your teacher read part A (phrasal verb and sentence), and create part B yourself without looking at the text. Repeat until you can speak smoothly.

EXAMPLE

put up . . . The rental company plans to deliver the wedding tent at 8:00 a.m.
A) "put up . . . The rental company plans to deliver the wedding tent at 8:00 a.m."
B) "Are they going to put it up?"

A)

1. cool off . . . They were sweating a lot after their long, hot hike.

2. leave behind . . . I can't find my umbrella, but I think I took it to work yesterday.

3. mess up . . . He wasn't prepared for his driver's license test, but he decided to take it.

4. put up . . . The rental company plans to deliver the wedding tent at 8:00 a.m.

5. come over . . . My son's piano teacher wants to see our piano and tune it for us.

6. sign up . . . She found a great online German language course.

7. take out . . . My contacts are bothering my eyes.

8. cheer up . . . They lost their baseball game, but the coach gave them a pep talk.

9. go away . . . I had a headache all morning.

10. line up . . . She recommended three more artists for our art exhibition next month.

Step 3: "No Hint"

Listen to your teacher read part A **without** the phrasal verb and create part B yourself, remembering the phrasal verb from context. Repeat until you can speak smoothly.

EXAMPLE:

put up . . . The rental company plans to deliver the wedding tent at 8:00 a.m.
A) "The rental company plans to deliver the wedding tent at 8:00 a.m."
B) "Are they going to put it up?"

Step 4: Continue the Conversation!

Do Step 3 again but continue a short, back-and-forth conversation with your teacher or language partner.

EXAMPLE:

put up . . . The rental company plans to deliver the wedding tent at 8:00 a.m.
A) "The rental company plans to deliver the wedding tent at 8:00 a.m."
B) "Are they going to put it up?"
A) "I hope so, because I don't know how to put it up!"
B) "How big is the tent?"
A) "It's big enough to seat 120 people."

Self-Study

Step 1: Read the examples aloud to get used to the pattern, and then go to Step 2.

Step 2: Read part A aloud and then try to create part B without looking at the text. Check your answers with the answer key. Repeat until you can speak part B smoothly without looking at the text.

Step 3: Cover the phrasal verbs with your hand or a sheet of paper. Read part A aloud **without** the phrasal verb and then create part B without looking at the text. Try to remember each phrasal verb from context. Repeat until you can speak smoothly and without hesitation.

Step 4: Do step 3 again but continue a short, back-and-forth imaginary conversation. Practice while speaking aloud.

CHAPTER

1. stay up
2. pack up
3. check out
4. take down
5. make sure
6. put back
7. take up
8. calm down
9. get lost
10. hang up

THE GOAL of this activity is to learn the meaning of each phrasal verb through context. Change the original sentence into a new, more natural sentence using the phrasal verb. Try to keep the sentences as similar as possible and change the phrasal verb form if necessary.

Step 1: Shadowing

Listen to your teacher read parts A and B aloud, and repeat each sentence without looking at the text (the teacher may use the answer key). If you need to glance at the text, use part A (below).

Step 2: Independent Response

Next, listen to your teacher read part A (phrasal verb and sentence), and create part B yourself without looking at the text. Repeat until you can speak smoothly.

EXAMPLE

take up . . . She plans to start learning golf when she retires.
A) "take up . . . She plans to start learning golf when she retires."
B) "She plans to take up golf when she retires."

A)

1. stay up . . . My kids always stay awake until midnight.

2. pack up . . . We should gather and pack our camping gear.

3. check out . . . She wants to pay the cashier before the store closes.

4. take down . . . I always remove my holiday decorations in January.

5. make sure . . . Can you confirm we have hotel reservations?

6. put back . . . He told his son to place the cookies on the table again.

7. take up . . . She plans to start learning golf when she retires.

8. calm down . . . Their dog never becomes calm around new people.

9. get lost . . . I always lose my way in big cities.

10. hang up . . . He puts his school uniform on a hanger every night.

11. check out . . . I'd like to observe that private school before I enroll my daughter.

12. hang up . . . If a scammer calls you, you should end the call right away.

Step 3: "No Hint" and Extra Comment

Listen to your teacher read part A **without** the phrasal verb and create part B yourself, remembering the phrasal verb from context. Add an extra comment to make your answer longer, and repeat until you can speak smoothly.

EXAMPLE:

take up . . . She plans to start learning golf when she retires.
A) "She plans to start learning golf when she retires."
B) "She plans to take up golf when she retires. She doesn't have enough time now."

Step 4: Continue the Conversation!

Do Step 3 again but continue a short, back-and-forth conversation with your teacher or language partner.

EXAMPLE:

take up . . . She plans to start learning golf when she retires.
A) "She plans to start learning golf when she retires."
B) "She plans to take up golf when she retires. She doesn't have enough time now."
A) "Has she ever tried it before?"
B) "A few times, but she's never taken lessons."

Self-Study

Step 1: Read the examples aloud to get used to the pattern, and then go to Step 2.

Step 2: Read part A aloud and then try to create part B without looking at the text. Check your answers with the answer key. Repeat until you can speak part B smoothly without looking at the text.

Step 3: Cover the phrasal verbs with your hand or a sheet of paper. Read part A aloud **without** the phrasal verb and then create part B without looking at the text. Try to remember each phrasal verb from context. Add an extra comment to make your answer longer.

Step 4: Do step 3 again but continue a short, back-and-forth imaginary conversation. Practice while speaking aloud.

9.2 QUICK ANSWERS
Answer questions quickly and naturally

THE GOAL of this activity is to give a quick, short answer using a phrasal verb in conversation. Use past tense and use "it/them" to keep your answer short and natural.

Step 1: Shadowing
Listen to your teacher read parts A and B aloud, and repeat each sentence without looking at the text (the teacher may use the answer key). If you need to glance at the text, use part A (below).

Step 2: Independent Response
Next, listen to your teacher read part A (phrasal verb and sentence), and create part B yourself without looking at the text. Repeat until you can speak smoothly.

EXAMPLE
put back . . . Did you replace those books on the shelf when you were finished?
A) "put back . . . Did you replace those books on the shelf when you were finished?"
B) "I put them back."

A)

1. stay up . . . Did he stay awake late last night?

2. pack up . . . Did they gather and pack the leftover food after the party?

3. check out . . . Did she go to see that new cafe?

4. take down . . . Did you dismantle your tent before leaving your campsite?

5. make sure . . . Did he check and confirm that the kids are asleep?

6. put back . . . Did you replace those books on the shelf when you were finished?

7. take up . . . Did she start doing yoga last year?

8. calm down . . . Did the kids become calm after the earthquake?

9. get lost . . . Did they lose their way at the airport?

10. hang up . . . Did he end his phone call with that telemarketer?

Step 3: "No Hint" and Extra Comment

Listen to your teacher read part A **without** the phrasal verb and create part B yourself, remembering the phrasal verb from context. Add an extra comment to make your answer longer, and repeat until you can speak smoothly.

EXAMPLE:
put back . . . Did you replace those books on the shelf when you were finished?
A) "Did you replace those books on the shelf when you were finished?"
B) "I put them back. They're my father's favorite books, so I have to be careful."

Step 4: Continue the Conversation!

Do Step 3 again but continue a short, back-and-forth conversation with your teacher or language partner.

EXAMPLE:
put back . . . Did you replace those books on the shelf when you were finished?
A) "Did you replace those books on the shelf when you were finished?"
B) "I put them back. They're my father's favorite books, so I have to be careful."
A) "Does he care if you borrow his books?"
B) "He doesn't mind . . . if I put them back when I'm done!"

Self-Study

Step 1: Read the examples aloud to get used to the pattern, and then go to Step 2.

Step 2: Read part A aloud and then try to create part B without looking at the text. Check your answers with the answer key. Repeat until you can speak part B smoothly without looking at the text.

Step 3: Cover the phrasal verbs with your hand or a sheet of paper. Read part A aloud **without** the phrasal verb and then create part B without looking at the text. Try to remember each phrasal verb from context. Add an extra comment to make your answer longer.

Step 4: Do step 3 again but continue a short, back-and-forth imaginary conversation. Practice while speaking aloud.

9.3 QUICK BUILDER
Quickly build more detailed answers

THE GOAL of this activity is to add more detail to your answer quickly with an extra verb. Follow the pattern (verb + to + phrasal verb) and create a past or future tense answer. Use "it/them" for a short, natural response.

Step 1: Shadowing

Listen to your teacher read parts A and B aloud, and repeat each sentence without looking at the text (the teacher may use the answer key). If you need to glance at the text, use part A (below).

Step 2: Independent Response

Next, listen to your teacher read part A (extra verb and sentence), and create part B yourself without looking at the text. Repeat until you can speak smoothly.

EXAMPLE
plan . . . Are you going to check out that new apartment?
A) "plan . . . Are you going to check out that new apartment?"
B) "I plan to check it out."

A)

1. plan . . . Are they going to stay up for the midnight movie showing?

2. decide . . . Did he already pack up all his ski gear?

3. plan . . . Are you going to check out that new apartment?

4. decide not . . . Did that celebrity take down his social media post?

5. promise . . . Is she going to make sure your cats are okay while you're gone?

6. forget . . . Did they put the lawnmower back in the garage?

7. hope . . . Are you going to take up piano this year?

8. try . . . Did he calm down his hyper kids at the restaurant?

9. happen . . . Did she get lost on her way to the restaurant?

10. remember . . . Did you hang up the wet towels in the bathroom?

Step 3: "No Hint" and Extra Comment

Listen to your teacher read part A **without** the extra verb and create part B yourself, remembering the verb from before. Add an extra comment to make your answer longer, and repeat until you can speak smoothly.

EXAMPLE:

plan . . . Are you going to check out that new apartment?
A) "Are you going to check out that new apartment?"
B) "I plan to check it out. I really want to move this spring!"

Step 4: Continue the Conversation!

Do Step 3 again but continue a short, back-and-forth conversation with your teacher or language partner.

EXAMPLE:

plan . . . Are you going to check out that new apartment?
A) "Are you going to check out that new apartment?"
B) "I plan to check it out. I really want to move this spring!"
A) "What's wrong with your apartment?"
B) "It's just too small, and I can hear my neighbors through the walls."

Self-Study

Step 1: Read the examples aloud to get used to the pattern, and then go to Step 2.

Step 2: Read part A aloud and then try to create part B without looking at the text. Check your answers with the answer key. Repeat until you can speak part B smoothly without looking at the text.

Step 3: Cover the extra verbs with your hand or a sheet of paper. Read part A aloud **without** the extra verb and then create part B without looking at the text. Try to remember the verb from before. Add an extra comment to make your answer longer.

Step 4: Do step 3 again but continue a short, back-and-forth imaginary conversation. Practice while speaking aloud.

9.4 QUICK QUESTIONS
Quickly ask questions to keep the conversation going

THE GOAL of this activity is to improve your small-talk skills by quickly asking a relevant question to keep the conversation going. Remember, being good at small talk means being good at asking questions! Use "it/them" and create a past or future tense question to match the situation.

Step 1: Shadowing

Listen to your teacher read parts A and B aloud, and repeat each sentence without looking at the text (the teacher may use the answer key). If you need to glance at the text, use part A (below).

Step 2: Independent Response

Next, listen to your teacher read part A (phrasal verb and sentence), and create part B yourself without looking at the text. Repeat until you can speak smoothly.

EXAMPLE

get lost . . . I took the wrong train at Tokyo Station this morning.
A) "get lost . . . I took the wrong train at Tokyo Station this morning."
B) "Did you get lost?"

A)

1. stay up . . . He planned to watch the Olympics at 1:00 a.m.

2. pack up . . . She wants to take all her old clothes to the secondhand shop.

3. check out . . . My kids really want to go to that new amusement park.

4. take down . . . The construction crew put up roadblocks on my street last month.

5. make sure . . . I asked him to confirm that there are vegan options at the restaurant.

6. put back . . . I asked her to put the car in the garage after she borrowed it.

7. take up . . . My son is crazy about surfing, but he's never tried it before.

8. calm down . . . His grandkids were too excited to go to bed.

9. get lost . . . I took the wrong train at Tokyo Station this morning.

10. hang up . . . She has been on the phone with a telemarketer for the past 20 minutes.

Step 3: "No Hint"

Listen to your teacher read part A **without** the phrasal verb and create part B yourself, remembering the phrasal verb from context. Repeat until you can speak smoothly.

EXAMPLE:
get lost . . . I took the wrong train at Tokyo Station this morning.
A) "I took the wrong train at Tokyo Station this morning."
B) "Did you get lost?"

Step 4: Continue the Conversation!

Do Step 3 again but continue a short, back-and-forth conversation with your teacher or language partner.

EXAMPLE:
get lost . . . I took the wrong train at Tokyo Station this morning.
A) "I took the wrong train at Tokyo Station this morning."
B) "Did you get lost?"
A) "Yeah, I was confused for a while, but then I figured it out."
B) "Were you late for work?"
A) "I have a flexible schedule, so it was no problem."

Self-Study

Step 1: Read the examples aloud to get used to the pattern, and then go to Step 2.

Step 2: Read part A aloud and then try to create part B without looking at the text. Check your answers with the answer key. Repeat until you can speak part B smoothly without looking at the text.

Step 3: Cover the phrasal verbs with your hand or a sheet of paper. Read part A aloud **without** the phrasal verb and then create part B without looking at the text. Try to remember each phrasal verb from context. Repeat until you can speak smoothly and without hesitation.

Step 4: Do step 3 again but continue a short, back-and-forth imaginary conversation. Practice while speaking aloud.

CHAPTER

10

1. go over

2. believe in

3. clear up

4. shut down

5. give up (on)

6. move in(to)

7. hang on(to)

8. put together

9. stay away (from)

10. think about

Quickly change regular sentences into phrasal-verb sentences

THE GOAL of this activity is to learn the meaning of each phrasal verb through context. Change the original sentence into a new, more natural sentence using the phrasal verb. Try to keep the sentences as similar as possible and change the phrasal verb form if necessary.

Step 1: Shadowing

Listen to your teacher read parts A and B aloud, and repeat each sentence without looking at the text (the teacher may use the answer key). If you need to glance at the text, use part A (below).

Step 2: Independent Response

Next, listen to your teacher read part A (phrasal verb and sentence), and create part B yourself without looking at the text. Repeat until you can speak smoothly.

EXAMPLE

move into . . . I want to start living in my new apartment soon.
A) "move into . . . I want to start living in my new apartment soon."
B) "I want to move into my new apartment soon."

A)

1. go over . . . He always explains the instructions multiple times.

2. believe in . . . Do you believe that ghosts are real?

3. clear up . . . She resolves many issues at work.

4. shut down . . . The company stopped doing business in January.

5. give up . . . He wants to quit smoking.

6. move into . . . I want to start living in my new apartment soon.

7. hang on . . . I'm busy, so could you wait for a moment?

8. put together . . . She often organizes presentations at work.

9. stay away from . . . I avoid dangerous areas in the city.

10. think about . . . It's important for students to consider their future careers.

11. hang onto . . . These stairs are steep, so you should keep holding the railing.

12. believe in . . . He believes that his country's Olympic team will do well.

13. clear up . . . The weather will become clear tomorrow.

14. go over . . . She plans to have an editor carefully check her scientific article.

A) Continued

15. put together . . . His son loves to assemble puzzles.

16. hang onto . . . Did you decide to keep your old car for a while?

Step 3: "No Hint" and Extra Comment

Listen to your teacher read part A **without** the phrasal verb and create part B yourself, remembering the phrasal verb from context. Add an extra comment to make your answer longer, and repeat until you can speak smoothly.

EXAMPLE:
move into . . . I want to start living in my new apartment soon.
A) "I want to start living in my new apartment soon."
B) "I want to move into my new apartment soon. I'm really looking forward to it!"

Step 4: Continue the Conversation!

Do Step 3 again but continue a short, back-and-forth conversation with your teacher or language partner.

EXAMPLE:
move into . . . I want to start living in my new apartment soon.
A) "I want to start living in my new apartment soon."
B) "I want to move into my new apartment soon. I'm really looking forward to it!"
A) "Where is your new apartment?"
B) "It's on 5th Street near that Italian restaurant we used to go to."

Self-Study

Step 1: Read the examples aloud to get used to the pattern, and then go to Step 2.

Step 2: Read part A aloud and then try to create part B without looking at the text. Check your answers with the answer key. Repeat until you can speak part B smoothly without looking at the text.

Step 3: Cover the phrasal verbs with your hand or a sheet of paper. Read part A aloud **without** the phrasal verb and then create part B without looking at the text. Try to remember each phrasal verb from context. Add an extra comment to make your answer longer.

Step 4: Do step 3 again but continue a short, back-and-forth imaginary conversation. Practice while speaking aloud.

THE GOAL of this activity is to give a quick, short answer using a phrasal verb in conversation. Use past tense and use "it/them" to keep your answer short and natural.

Step 1: Shadowing

Listen to your teacher read parts A and B aloud, and repeat each sentence without looking at the text (the teacher may use the answer key). If you need to glance at the text, use part A (below).

Step 2: Independent Response

Next, listen to your teacher read part A (phrasal verb and sentence), and create part B yourself without looking at the text. Repeat until you can speak smoothly.

EXAMPLE

hang onto . . . Did you decide to keep your old piano?
A) "hang onto . . . Did you decide to keep your old piano?"
B) "I hung onto it."

A)

1. go over . . . Did he examine your report?

2. believe in . . . Do they have confidence that she will become a famous musician?

3. clear up . . . Did the sky become clear after the rain?

4. shut down . . . Did the owner close his restaurant during Covid?

5. give up on . . . Did she stop trying to become a YouTube star?

6. move in . . . Did they transport all their furniture to their new house?

7. hang onto . . . Did you decide to keep your old piano?

8. put together . . . Did the kids assemble their new Lego set?

9. stay away from . . . Did he avoid his coworkers yesterday?

10. think about . . . Did she carefully consider changing jobs?

Step 3: "No Hint" and Extra Comment

Listen to your teacher read part A **without** the phrasal verb and create part B yourself, remembering the phrasal verb from context. Add an extra comment to make your answer longer, and repeat until you can speak smoothly.

EXAMPLE:

hang onto . . . Did you decide to keep your old piano?
A) "Did you decide to keep your old piano?"
B) "I hung onto it. My daughter said she might want to try piano lessons."

Step 4: Continue the Conversation!

Do Step 3 again but continue a short, back-and-forth conversation with your teacher or language partner.

EXAMPLE:

hang onto . . . Did you decide to keep your old piano?
A) "Did you decide to keep your old piano?"
B) "I hung onto it. My daughter said she might want to try piano lessons."
A) "How old is your daughter?"
B) "She's just four, but I think I'll sign her up for piano lessons next year."

Self-Study

Step 1: Read the examples aloud to get used to the pattern, and then go to Step 2.

Step 2: Read part A aloud and then try to create part B without looking at the text. Check your answers with the answer key. Repeat until you can speak part B smoothly without looking at the text.

Step 3: Cover the phrasal verbs with your hand or a sheet of paper. Read part A aloud **without** the phrasal verb and then create part B without looking at the text. Try to remember each phrasal verb from context. Add an extra comment to make your answer longer.

Step 4: Do step 3 again but continue a short, back-and-forth imaginary conversation. Practice while speaking aloud.

THE GOAL of this activity is to add more detail to your answer quickly with an extra verb. Follow the pattern (verb + to + phrasal verb) and create a past or future tense answer. Use "it/them" for a short, natural response.

Step 1: Shadowing

Listen to your teacher read parts A and B aloud, and repeat each sentence without looking at the text (the teacher may use the answer key). If you need to glance at the text, use part A (below).

Step 2: Independent Response

Next, listen to your teacher read part A (extra verb and sentence), and create part B yourself without looking at the text. Repeat until you can speak smoothly.

EXAMPLE

decide not . . . Did you give up on your dream of becoming a doctor?
A) "decide not . . . Did you give up on your dream of becoming a doctor?"
B) "I decided not to give up on it."

A)

1. forget . . . Did the teacher go over that recipe in cooking class?

2. try . . . Did you believe in your brother's new business idea?

3. hope . . . Is he going to clear up the argument between his children?

4. plan . . . Are they going to shut down their factory in Mexico?

5. decide not . . . Did you give up on your dream of becoming a doctor?

6. decide . . . Is she going to move in with her parents?

7. forget . . . Did you hang onto your old school yearbooks?

8. want . . . Is she going to put that Ikea shelf together?

9. promise . . . Did the kids stay away from the park last night?

10. refuse . . . Did he think about moving back to California?

Step 3: "No Hint" and Extra Comment

Listen to your teacher read part A **without** the extra verb and create part B yourself, remembering the verb from before. Add an extra comment to make your answer longer, and repeat until you can speak smoothly.

EXAMPLE:
decide not . . . Did you give up on your dream of becoming a doctor?
A) "Did you give up on your dream of becoming a doctor?"
B) "I decided not to give up on it. Medical school is expensive, though!"

Step 4: Continue the Conversation!

Do Step 3 again but continue a short, back-and-forth conversation with your teacher or language partner.

EXAMPLE:
decide not . . . Did you give up on your dream of becoming a doctor?
A) "Did you give up on your dream of becoming a doctor?"
B) "I decided not to give up on it. Medical school is expensive, though!"
A) "Can you get any scholarships?"
B) "I've applied for some scholarships, but I'll need to take out some loans, too."

Self-Study

Step 1: Read the examples aloud to get used to the pattern, and then go to Step 2.

Step 2: Read part A aloud and then try to create part B without looking at the text. Check your answers with the answer key. Repeat until you can speak part B smoothly without looking at the text.

Step 3: Cover the extra verbs with your hand or a sheet of paper. Read part A aloud **without** the extra verb and then create part B without looking at the text. Try to remember the verb from before. Add an extra comment to make your answer longer.

Step 4: Do step 3 again but continue a short, back-and-forth imaginary conversation. Practice while speaking aloud.

THE GOAL of this activity is to improve your small-talk skills by quickly asking a relevant question to keep the conversation going. Remember, being good at small talk means being good at asking questions! Use "it/them" and create a past or future tense question to match the situation.

Step 1: Shadowing

Listen to your teacher read parts A and B aloud, and repeat each sentence without looking at the text (the teacher may use the answer key). If you need to glance at the text, use part A (below).

Step 2: Independent Response

Next, listen to your teacher read part A (phrasal verb and sentence), and create part B yourself without looking at the text. Repeat until you can speak smoothly.

EXAMPLE

clear up . . . My boss says she will explain our confusing new remote-work policy.
A) "clear up . . . My boss says she will explain our confusing new remote-work policy."
B) "Is she going to clear it up?"

A)

1. go over . . . I asked him to check my PowerPoint presentation for mistakes.

2. believe in . . . When I was a kid, my brother told me that vampires are real.

3. clear up . . . My boss says she will explain our confusing new remote-work policy.

4. shut down . . . The rail company was worried about running trains during the storm.

5. give up . . . He thinks eating red meat is unhealthy and bad for the environment.

6. move into . . . Her company gave her a big, private office.

7. hang onto . . . I was walking my dog, and he tried to chase a stray cat.

8. put together . . . My neighbor bought a new gas grill, but she hasn't assembled it yet.

9. stay away . . . His in-laws told him not to visit, because they had the flu.

10. think about . . . Her company wants her to move to New York City.

Step 3: "No Hint"

Listen to your teacher read part A **without** the phrasal verb and create part B yourself, remembering the phrasal verb from context. Repeat until you can speak smoothly.

EXAMPLE:
clear up . . . My boss says she will explain our confusing new remote-work policy.
A) "My boss says she will explain our confusing new remote-work policy."
B) "Is she going to clear it up?"

Step 4: Continue the Conversation!

Do Step 3 again but continue a short, back-and-forth conversation with your teacher or language partner.

EXAMPLE:
clear up . . . My boss says she will explain our confusing new remote-work policy.
A) "My boss says she will explain our confusing new remote-work policy."
B) "Is she going to clear it up?"
A) "I hope so! Everyone is confused and worried about it."
B) "Do most of your colleagues work from home?"
A) "Everyone does. I hope that doesn't change."

Self-Study

Step 1: Read the examples aloud to get used to the pattern, and then go to Step 2.

Step 2: Read part A aloud and then try to create part B without looking at the text. Check your answers with the answer key. Repeat until you can speak part B smoothly without looking at the text.

Step 3: Cover the phrasal verbs with your hand or a sheet of paper. Read part A aloud **without** the phrasal verb and then create part B without looking at the text. Try to remember each phrasal verb from context. Repeat until you can speak smoothly and without hesitation.

Step 4: Do step 3 again but continue a short, back-and-forth imaginary conversation. Practice while speaking aloud.

ANSWER KEYS

1.1 Answer Key

1. A) figure out . . . I solve a lot of problems at work.
    B) I figure out a lot of problems at work.

2. A) put off . . . We often postpone meetings when we're busy.
    B) We often put off meetings when we're busy.
    /or/ We often put meetings off when we're busy.

3. A) heat up . . . If we don't have time to cook, we can warm some food in the microwave.
    B) If we don't have time to cook, we can heat up some food in the microwave.
    /or/ If we don't have time to cook, we can heat some food up in the microwave.

4. A) get together . . . We meet at the café once a week.
    B) We get together at the café once a week.

5. A) throw away . . . She wants to discard her old clothes.
    B) She wants to throw away her old clothes.
    /or/ She wants to throw her old clothes away.

6. A) come down with . . . He catches a cold every winter.
    B) He comes down with a cold every winter.

7. A) look over . . . She carefully examines all her bank statements.
    B) She carefully looks over all her bank statements.
    /or/ She carefully looks all her bank statements over.

8. A) clean up . . . He's a messy cook, so he has to clean the kitchen after cooking.
    B) He's a messy cook, so he has to clean up the kitchen after cooking.
    /or/ He's a messy cook, so he has to clean the kitchen up after cooking.

9. A) run into . . . I'm worried that I will suddenly meet my old boss at the station.
    B) I'm worried that I will run into my old boss at the station.

10. A) take over . . . He's sick, so could you lead his presentation?
    B) He's sick, so could you take over his presentation?

11. A) run into . . . The sidewalk is crowded, so please try not to hit people with your bike.
    B) The sidewalk is crowded, so please try not to run into people with your bike.

1.2 Answer Key

1. A) figure out . . . Did you discover how to create your own YouTube channel?
    B) I figured it out.

2. A) put off . . . Did they postpone their party?
    B) They put it off.

3. A) heat up . . . Did he warm that cold soup before eating it?
    B) He heated it up.

4. A) get together . . . Did you and your uncle meet last week?
    B) We got together.

5. A) throw away . . . Did he discard his old laptop?
    B) He threw it away.

6. A) come down with . . . Did she get the flu?
    B) She came down with it.

7. A) look over . . . Did you take a look at the online schedule?
    B) I looked it over.

8. A) clean up . . . Did your son tidy his bedroom?
    B) He cleaned it up.

9. A) run into . . . Did you see our new clients at the conference?
    B) I ran into them.

10. A) take over . . . Did she take control of the project?
    B) She took it over.

1.3 Answer Key

1. A) try . . . Did she figure out the printer problem?
    B) She tried to figure it out.

2. A) want . . . Is he going to put off the presentation?
    B) He wants to put it off.

3. A) forget . . . Did you heat up the pasta for dinner?
    B) I forgot to heat it up.

4. A) plan . . . Are they going to get together soon?
    B) They plan to get together.

5. A) decide not . . . Did you throw away your old skis?
    B) I decided not to throw them away.

6. A) happen . . . Did he come down with the flu?
    B) He happened to come down with it.

7. A) promise . . . Is she going to look over your resume?
    B) She promised to look it over.

8. A) decide . . . Did he clean up the living room?
    B) He decided to clean it up.

9. A) hope . . . Did they run into her at the park?
    B) They happened to run into her.

10. A) agree . . . Did you take over the book club when your leader quit?
    B) I agreed to take it over.

1.4 Answer Key

1.   A) figure out . . . He tried to find his way to the cafe.
        B) Did he figure it out?

2.   A) put off . . . They want to postpone their wedding.
        B) Are they going to put it off?

3.   A) heat up . . . I drank the old coffee instead of making more.
        B) Did you heat it up?

4.   A) get together . . . We want to spend time together next week.
        B) Are you going to get together?

5.   A) throw away . . . I got rid of my old sofa.
        B) Did you throw it away?

6.   A) come down with . . . He was worried his daughter would catch Covid.
        B) Did she come down with it?

7.   A) look over . . . He wants her to check his resume.
        B) Is she going to look it over?

8.   A) clean up . . . She asked them to clean and organize the conference room.
        B) Did they clean it up?

9.   A) run into . . . I wanted to see my old high school friend at the reunion.
        B) Did you run into him/her?

10.   A) take over . . . She might be in charge of the cooking class when our teacher retires.
        B) Is she going to take it over?
        /or/ Is she going to take over?

2.1 Answer Key

1. A) give away . . . She donates her old clothes to the secondhand shop.
   B) She gives away her old clothes to the secondhand shop.
   /or/ She gives her old clothes away to the secondhand shop.

2. A) take care of . . . When her brother travels, she cares for his dog.
   B) When her brother travels, she takes care of his dog.

3. A) put away . . . He always puts his clean laundry in the closet.
   B) He always puts his clean laundry away.
   /or/ He always puts away his clean laundry.

4. A) ask over . . . He invites his friends to his house every weekend.
   B) He asks his friends over every weekend.

5. A) go up . . . I hope food prices don't increase this year.
   B) I hope food prices don't go up this year.

6. A) pick up . . . I usually get groceries after work.
   B) I usually pick up groceries after work.
   /or/ I usually pick groceries up after work.

7. A) sleep in . . . I sleep late on Saturday mornings.
   B) I sleep in on Saturday mornings.

8. A) put on . . . We need to dress in warm clothes before we go out in the blizzard.
   B) We need to put on warm clothes before we go out in the blizzard.
   /or/ We need to put warm clothes on before we go out in the blizzard.

9. A) work on . . . I should spend time doing my tax paperwork this month.
   B) I should work on my tax paperwork this month.

10. A) hang out . . . They usually spend time together at the park.
    B) They usually hang out at the park.
    /or/ They usually hang out together at the park.

11. A) take care of . . . I don't have time, so can you handle that new project yourself?
    B) I don't have time, so can you take care of that new project yourself?
    /or/ I don't have time, so can you take care of that new project?

12. A) pick up . . . He asked his brother to go and get the kids from school.
    B) He asked his brother to pick up the kids from school.
    /or/ He asked his brother to pick the kids up from school.

13. A) put on . . . She asked her son to clean up his books and place them on his shelf.
    B) She asked her son to clean up his books and put them on his shelf.

2.2 Answer Key

1. A) give away . . . Did you give your prize money to someone else after the contest?
    B) I gave it away.

2. A) take care of . . . Did he look after the kids?
    B) He took care of them.

3. A) put away . . . Did she put the car in the garage?
    B) She put it away.

4. A) ask over . . . Did you invite your aunt to your house?
    B) I asked her over.

5. A) go up . . . Did your rent increase last year?
    B) It went up.

6. A) pick up . . . Did he get milk on his way home?
    B) He picked it up.
    /or/ He picked some up.

7. A) sleep in . . . Did she sleep late this morning?
    B) She slept in.

8. A) put on . . . Did you wear your motorcycle helmet?
    B) I put it on.

9. A) work on . . . Did you practice your speech?
    B) I worked on it.

10. A) hang out . . . Did they spend time at the beach?
    B) They hung out.
    /or/ They hung out there.

2.3 Answer Key

1. A) decide . . . Did she give away those concert tickets?
   B) She decided to give them away.

2. A) promise . . . Is he going to take care of this mess?
   B) He promised to take care of it.
   /or/ He promises to take care of it.

3. A) forget . . . Did you put away your bike?
   B) I forgot to put it away.

4. A) plan . . . Are they going to ask their neighbors over?
   B) They plan to ask them over.

5. A) happen . . . Did his tuition go up?
   B) It happened to go up.

6. A) decide not . . . Did he pick up groceries?
   B) He decided not to pick them up.

7. A) hope . . . Is she going to sleep in this weekend?
   B) She hopes to sleep in.

8. A) forget . . . Did she put on sunscreen at the beach?
   B) She forgot to put it on.

9. A) agree . . . Did they work on their company's website design?
   B) They agreed to work on it.

10. A) want . . . Are you going to hang out with your coworkers at the party?
    B) I want to hang out with them.
    /or/ We want to hang out.

2.4 Answer Key

1. A) give away . . . I'm not going to keep those movie tickets.
    B) Are you going to give them away?

2. A) take care of . . . My neighbor asked me to look after her cat last weekend.
    B) Did you take care of it/him/her?

3. A) put away . . . She asked her son to put the lawnmower in the garage.
    B) Did he put it away?

4. A) ask over . . . I wanted to invite my friends to my house for dinner.
    B) Did you ask them over?

5. A) go up . . . I was worried my son's fever would get higher.
    B) Did it go up?

6. A) pick up . . . She asked him to come and get her from the station.
    B) Did he pick her up?

7. A) sleep in . . . I hope to get lots of sleep this weekend.
    B) Are you going to sleep in?

8. A) put on . . . He told his daughter to wear her seatbelt on her road trip.
    B) Did she put it on?

9. A) work on . . . I need to practice and improve my English this year.
    B) Are you going to work on it?

10. A) hang out . . . They wanted to spend time together last Sunday.
    B) Did they hang out?
    /or/ Did they hang out together?

3.1 Answer Key

1. A) get rid of . . . She often deletes the old photos on her phone.
    B) She often gets rid of the old photos on her phone.

2. A) look into . . . The police investigate a lot of crimes every year.
    B) The police look into a lot of crimes every year.

3. A) think over . . . He thinks carefully about every decision.
    B) He thinks over every decision (carefully).
    /or/ He thinks every decision over (carefully).

4. A) work out . . . She solves a lot of interpersonal problems in the office.
    B) She works out a lot of interpersonal problems in the office.

5. A) get along with . . . I have a good relationship with my coworkers.
    B) I get along with my coworkers.

6. A) try on . . . I always put on jeans to check the fit before buying them.
    B) I always try on jeans before buying them.
    /or/ I always try jeans on before buying them.

7. A) come back . . . They always return from trips with too many souvenirs.
    B) They always come back from trips with too many souvenirs.

8. A) turn on . . . You should start the electric heater.
    B) You should turn on the electric heater.
    /or/ You should turn the electric heater on.

9. A) look for . . . Every morning I search for my glasses.
    B) Every morning I look for my glasses.

10. A) clean out . . . It's time to clean and remove things from your garage.
    B) It's time to clean out your garage.
    /or/ It's time to clean your garage out.

11. A) look into . . . I decided to find more information about art classes for my daughter.
    B) I decided to look into art classes for my daughter.

3.2 Answer Key

1. A) get rid of . . . Did she throw away the receipt?
    B) She got rid of it.

2. A) look into . . . Did they investigate their Wi-Fi problem?
    B) They looked into it.

3. A) think over . . . Did he think carefully about the job offer?
    B) He thought it over.

4. A) work out . . . Did you fix your schedule conflict?
    B) I worked it out.

5. A) get along with . . . Did you enjoy working with your new colleague?
    B) I got along with him/her.

6. A) try on . . . Did he put on those ski boots to check the fit?
    B) He tried them on.

7. A) come back . . . Did they already return from their trip?
    B) They came back.

8. A) turn on . . . Did you start up your computer?
    B) I turned it on.

9. A) look for . . . Did she search for her phone?
    B) She looked for it.

10. A) clean out . . . Did they clean and remove things from their office?
    B) They cleaned it out.
    /or/ They cleaned them out.

3.3 Answer Key

1. A) decide . . . Did you get rid of the leftover food in your fridge?
   B) I decided to get rid of it.

2. A) agree . . . Did she look into our company's website issue?
   B) She agreed to look into it.

3. A) promise . . . Are you going to think over my YouTube idea?
   B) I promise to think it over.

4. A) hope . . . Are they going to work out a time to meet?
   B) They hope to work it out.

5. A) seem . . . Did he get along with his homestay family?
   B) He seemed to get along with them.

6. A) decide not . . . Did he try on that expensive leather jacket?
   B) He decided not to try it on.

7. A) hope . . . Are they going to come back to Japan?
   B) They hope to come back.

8. A) forget . . . Did she turn on her home alarm system?
   B) She forgot to turn it on.

9. A) remember . . . Did he look for that important email from his boss?
   B) He remembered to look for it.

10. A) plan . . . Are you going to clean out your car this weekend?
    B) I plan to clean it out.

3.4 Answer Key

1. A) get rid of . . . I don't want to keep my old car because it has too many issues.
   B) Are you going to get rid of it?

2. A) look into . . . He wants to gather more information on that scholarship program.
   B) Is he going to look into it?

3. A) think over . . . She can't decide whether or not to attend their wedding in Hawaii.
   B) Is she going to think it over?
   /or/ Is she thinking it over?

4. A) work out . . . They struggled to create a new social media plan for their company.
   B) Did they work it out?

5. A) get along . . . I hope my dogs can spend time together next weekend without fighting.
   B) Are they going to get along?
   /or/ Do you think they'll get along?

6. A) try on . . . He looked at five different pairs of shoes at the store.
   B) Did he try them on?
   /or/ Did he try any on?

7. A) come back . . . She wanted to return home early from Paris.
   B) Did she come back?
   /or/ Did she come back early?

8. A) turn on . . . He asked them to activate the alarm system when they left the house.
   B) Did they turn it on?

9. A) look for . . . She asked me to help her find her keys.
   B) Did you look for them?

10. A) clean out . . . I should clean and remove everything from my kitchen cupboards.
    B) Are you going to clean them out?

4.1 Answer Key

1. A) look after . . . He needs to take care of his brother's kids.
    B) He needs to look after his brother's kids.

2. A) come up with . . . I usually think of good ideas in the morning.
    B) I usually come up with good ideas in the morning.

3. A) get over . . . She always recovers from colds quickly.
    B) She always gets over colds quickly.

4. A) fill out . . . You need to complete this application by adding information.
    B) You need to fill out this application.
    /or/ You need to fill this application out.

5. A) try out . . . He wants to try using his new camera for the first time.
    B) He wants to try out his new camera.
    /or/ He wants to try his new camera out.

6. A) eat out . . . They eat at restaurants almost every night.
    B) They eat out almost every night.

7. A) call back . . . She usually returns calls right away.
    B) She usually calls back right away.

8. A) shop around . . . I always shop at multiple stores before buying anything.
    B) I always shop around before buying anything.

9. A) start over . . . He doesn't like to start movies from the beginning again.
    B) He doesn't like to start movies over.

10. A) come across . . . She often encounters road construction in Chicago.
    B) She often comes across road construction in Chicago.

11. A) come up with . . . She creates a new recipe for gluten-free bread every week.
    B) She comes up with a new recipe for gluten-free bread every week.

12. A) come across . . . I sometimes discover stray cats in my back yard.
    B) I sometimes come across stray cats in my back yard.

4.2 Answer Key

1. A) look after . . . Did he take care of his grandkids?
   B) He looked after them.

2. A) come up with . . . Did she create that new mobile app?
   B) She came up with it.

3. A) get over . . . Did he recover from losing his job?
   B) He got over it.

4. A) fill out . . . Did she complete the online form?
   B) She filled it out.

5. A) try out . . . Did they test their new tent before their big camping trip?
   B) They tried it out.

6. A) eat out . . . Did she eat at a restaurant yesterday?
   B) She ate out.
   /or/ She ate out yesterday.

7. A) call back . . . Did they return his call?
   B) They called him back.

8. A) shop around . . . Did he look in multiple stores?
   B) He shopped around.

9. A) start over . . . Did she start the project from the beginning again?
   B) She started it over.
   /or/ She started over.

10. A) come across . . . Did you discover those old books in your attic?
    B) I came across them.
    /or/ I came across them there.

4.3 Answer Key

1.   A) agree . . . Are you going to look after your friend's parrot?
     B) I agreed to look after it/him/her.

2.   A) forget . . . Did he come up with this week's video for his YouTube channel?
     B) He forgot to come up with it.

3.   A) seem . . . Did they get over their argument?
     B) They seemed to get over it.

4.   A) decide not . . . Did you fill out the gym membership form?
     B) I decided not to fill it out.

5.   A) want . . . Is she going to try out those new ice skates?
     B) She wants to try them out.

6.   A) promise . . . Are they going to eat out with us this weekend?
     B) They promised to eat out with us.
     /or/ They promise to eat out with us.

7.   A) remember . . . Did you call your mom back?
     B) I remembered to call her back.

8.   A) hope . . . Is she going to shop around for a new car?
     B) She hopes to shop around.

9.   A) plan . . . Are you going to start that novel over?
     B) I plan to start it over.

10. A) happen . . . While he was in Paris, did he come across the bakery I recommended?
     B) He happened to come across it.

4.4 Answer Key

1. A) look after . . . They asked her to take care of their daughters next week.
    B) Is she going to look after them?

2. A) come up with . . . He told me about a new way to improve my golf swing.
    B) Did he come up with it?
    /or/ Did he come up with it himself?

3. A) get over . . . I had horrible allergies last spring.
    B) Did you get over them?

4. A) fill out . . . The employment agency gave her a dozen job applications.
    B) Did she fill them out?

5. A) try out . . . I just heard about a new social media app.
    B) Are you going to try it out?
    /or/ Did you try it out?

6. A) eat out . . . She doesn't want to cook at all this weekend.
    B) Is she going to eat out?

7. A) call back . . . My uncle left me a voicemail last week.
    B) Did you call him back?

8. A) shop around . . . They think their local electronics store is too expensive.
    B) Are they going to shop around?

9. A) start over . . . She just started her speech, but her microphone isn't working.
    B) Is she going to start over?

10. A) come across . . . He was hoping to find his missing laptop.
    B) Did he come across it?

5.1 Answer Key

1. A) ask out . . . He often asks her to go out to dinner with him.
    B) He often asks her out to dinner.

2. A) go back . . . She sometimes returns to the office at night.
    B) She sometimes goes back to the office at night.

3. A) drop by . . . He usually goes to the convenience store after work.
    B) He usually drops by the convenience store after work.

4. A) hand out . . . That store gives everyone free samples on weekends.
    B) That store hands out free samples on weekends.
    /or/ That store hands free samples out on weekends.

5. A) hang around . . . She likes to spend time at her friend's house on weeknights.
    B) She likes to hang around her friend's house on weeknights.
    /or/ She likes to hang around at her friend's house on weeknights.

6. A) close down . . . I hope that little restaurant doesn't close permanently.
    B) I hope that little restaurant doesn't close down.

7. A) check on . . . She always takes a look at her baby at night to make sure he's ok.
    B) She always checks on her baby at night.
    /or/ She always checks on her baby at night to make sure he's ok.

8. A) bring over . . . Can you bring some sandwiches to my house?
    B) Can you bring over some sandwiches?
    /or/ Can you bring some sandwiches over?

9. A) look around . . . You should explore the new park.
    B) You should look around the new park.

10. A) send back . . . He returns a lot of Amazon orders through the mail.
    B) He sends back a lot of Amazon orders.
    /or/ He sends a lot of Amazon orders back.

11. A) check on . . . At work, I often need to confirm the status of our inventory.
    B) At work, I often need to check on our inventory.

5.2 Answer Key

1. A) ask out . . . Did she ask her coworkers to go out for drinks with her?
   B) She asked them out.

2. A) go back . . . Did he return to the station to look for his iPhone?
   B) He went back.

3. A) drop by . . . Did they visit your house for a short time?
   B) They dropped by.

4. A) hand out . . . Did you distribute nametags to everyone?
   B) I handed them out.

5. A) hang around . . . Did he spend some extra time at the casino?
   B) He hung around.
   /or/ He hung around there.

6. A) close down . . . Did that company stop doing business?
   B) It closed down.
   /or/ They closed down.

7. A) check on . . . Did you check to see what the kids were doing?
   B) I checked on them.

8. A) bring over . . . Did she bring her laptop to your house?
   B) She brought it over.

9. A) look around . . . Did he explore Taipei on his business trip?
   B) He looked around.

10. A) send back . . . Did they return the clothes they ordered online?
    B) They sent them back.

5.3 Answer Key

1. A) plan . . . Are you going to ask them out to that Indian restaurant?
   B) I plan to ask them out.

2. A) agree . . . Did he go back to his parents' house last weekend?
   B) He agreed to go back.
   /or/ He agreed to go back there.

3. A) hope . . . Are you going to drop by the football game later?
   B) I hope to drop by.
   /or/ I hope to drop by there.

4. A) decide not . . . Did they hand out free bottled water at the race?
   B) They decided not to hand it out.

5. A) want . . . Did his daughter hang around the mall with her friends last night?
   B) She wanted to hang around.
   /or/ She wanted to hang around there.

6. A) appear . . . Did that electronics store close down for a while last year?
   B) It appeared to close down.

7. A) promise . . . Is he going to check on the turkey in the oven?
   B) He promised to check on it.
   /or/ He promises to check on it.

8. A) forget . . . Did she bring over her homework?
   B) She forgot to bring it over.

9. A) decide . . . Did the police look around the crime scene?
   B) They decided to look around.

10. A) remember . . . Did you send back the book you borrowed from your cousin?
    B) I remembered to send it back.
    /or/ I remembered to send it back to her/him.

5.4 Answer Key

1.   A) ask out . . . She wants to go to the school dance with him.
      B) Is she going to ask him out?

2.   A) go back . . . He planned to return to San Francisco last year.
      B) Did he go back?

3.   A) drop by . . . They told me they would stop at my house on their way to Chicago.
      B) Did they drop by?

4.   A) hand out . . . She has a lot of flyers to advertise her new business.
      B) Is she going to hand them out?

5.   A) hang around . . . We invited my son's friends to stay and play games after dinner.
      B) Did they hang around?

6.   A) close down . . . My favorite farmers market is struggling to make money.
      B) Is it going to close down?
      /or/ Are they going to close down?

7.   A) check on . . . His dog was barking a lot in the backyard.
      B) Did he check on it/him/her?

8.   A) bring over . . . I'm sick, and my neighbor just called to say she's making dinner for me.
      B) Is she going to bring it over?

9.   A) look around . . . I couldn't find a good cafe near my hotel.
      B) Did you look around?

10.   A) send back . . . Her new smart TV was just delivered, but it doesn't work.
      B) Is she going to send it back?

6.1 Answer Key

1. A) meet with . . . She often has a meeting with her boss on Fridays.
   B) She often meets with her boss on Fridays.

2. A) have over . . . I have my parents come to my house every Sunday.
   B) I have my parents over every Sunday.

3. A) get back . . . He returns home from work by 6 p.m.
   B) He gets back from work by 6 p.m.

4. A) go down . . . I hope the price of gas decreases.
   B) I hope the price of gas goes down.

5. A) send out . . . They always mail New Year's cards to all their friends.
   B) They always send out New Year's cards to all their friends.
   /or/ They always send New Year's cards out to all their friends.

6. A) let into . . . It's a little early, but I hope they let us enter the cafe.
   B) It's a little early, but I hope they let us into the cafe.

7. A) help out . . . She helps her team members at work.
   B) She helps out her team members at work.
   /or/ She helps her team members out at work.

8. A) shut off . . . Can you turn off the sink?
   B) Can you shut off the sink?
   /or/ Can you shut the sink off?

9. A) look up . . . I usually search for directions on my phone.
   B) I usually look up directions on my phone.
   /or/ I usually look directions up on my phone.

10. A) check into . . . I want to get more information about piano lessons for my son.
    B) I want to check into piano lessons for my son.

11. A) get back . . . Did she retrieve her lost purse?
    B) Did she get her lost purse back?
    /or/ Did she get back her lost purse?

12. A) let into . . . I love playing guitar, so I hope they allow me to join their band.
    B) I love playing guitar, so I hope they let me into their band.

6.2 Answer Key

1. A) meet with . . . Did you get together with your Dutch clients?
   B) I met with them.

2. A) have over . . . Did he invite his in-laws to his house?
   B) He had them over.

3. A) get back . . . Did she retrieve her lost iPhone?
   B) She got it back.

4. A) go down . . . Did the temperature drop last night?
   B) It went down.

5. A) send out . . . Did you send the new schedule in that group email?
   B) I sent it out.

6. A) let in . . . Did they allow him to join their football club?
   B) They let him in.

7. A) help out . . . Did the shop staff assist you?
   B) They helped me out.

8. A) shut off . . . Did she turn off the gas heater?
   B) She shut it off.

9. A) look up . . . Did you check those English words in the dictionary?
   B) I looked them up.

10. A) check into . . . Did he find more information about renting a car?
    B) He checked into it.

6.3 Answer Key

1. A) decide not . . . Did you meet with your professor last week?
    B) I decided not to meet with him/her.

2. A) plan . . . Is he going to have his photography club over?
    B) He plans to have them over.

3. A) try . . . Did you get your money back from email scam?
    B) I tried to get it back.

4. A) seem . . . Did your son's fever go down today?
    B) It seemed to go down.

5. A) remember . . . Did she send out those invitations?
    B) She remembered to send them out.

6. A) agree . . . Are they going to let customers into the gym before 6:00 a.m.?
    B) They agreed to let them in.

7. A) promise . . . Is she going to help out her nephew by donating to his fundraiser?
    B) She promised to help him out.

8. A) forget . . . Did you shut off the TV?
    B) I forgot to shut it off.

9. A) plan . . . Is he going to look up the instructions for that Ikea table?
    B) He plans to look them up.

10. A) decide . . . Did you check into that new budget airline?
    B) I decided to check into it.

6.4 Answer Key

1.   A) meet with . . . He considered scheduling an appointment with his therapist last week.
      B) Did he meet with him/her?

2.   A) have over . . . They want to have a barbecue party with their neighbors.
      B) Are they going to have them over?

3.   A) get back . . . My dry cleaner said he couldn't find my winter coat.
      B) Did you get it back?

4.   A) go down . . . I was hoping that house prices would decrease in Florida last year.
      B) Did they go down?

5.   A) send out . . . The company asked her to mail them a hard copy of her resume.
      B) Did she send it out?
      /or/ Did she send one out?

6.   A) let in . . . My dog is really muddy, but he wants to come into the house.
      B) Are you going to let him in?

7.   A) help out . . . Her brother asked her for financial help last year.
      B) Did she help him out?

8.   A) shut off . . . My neighbor's car alarm was going off early this morning.
      B) Did he/she shut it off?
      /or/ Did they shut it off?

9.   A) look up . . . He plans to cook paella, but he doesn't know how!
      B) Is he going to look it up?

10.   A) check into . . . She heard that she was eligible for a promotion.
      B) Did she check into it?

7.1 Answer Key

1. A) take off . . . I can't take vacation time from work in December.
    B) I can't take off from work in December.
    /or/ I can't take off work in December.
    /or/ I can't take off in December.

2. A) hand in . . . Did you submit your essay to the professor?
    B) Did you hand in your essay to the professor?
    /or/ Did you hand your essay in to the professor?

3. A) go out . . . They always go to the bars on weekends.
    B) They always go out on weekends.
    /or/ They always go out to the bars on weekends.

4. A) warm up . . . On cold days, you should heat your car before driving.
    B) On cold days, you should warm up your car before driving.
    /or/ On cold days, you should warm your car up before driving.

5. A) take back . . . He often returns clothes to the store.
    B) He often takes clothes back to the store.

6. A) look forward to . . . She always gets excited about her business trips.
    B) She always looks forward to her business trips.

7. A) set up . . . They love camping, and they can quickly construct their tent.
    B) They love camping, and they can quickly set up their tent.
    /or/ They love camping, and they can quickly set their tent up.

8. A) drop off (at) . . . I take my kids to school every morning.
    B) I drop off my kids at school every morning.
    /or/ I drop my kids off at school every morning.

9. A) wake up . . . He usually awakens at 6:00 a.m.
    B) He usually wakes up at 6:00 a.m.

10. A) turn down . . . She loves her company, so she always refuses other job offers.
    B) She loves her company, so she always turns down other job offers.
    /or/ She loves her company, so she always turns other job offers down.

11. A) take off . . . It's hot in here, so I need to remove my wool sweater.
    B) It's hot in here, so I need to take off my wool sweater.
    /or/ It's hot in here, so I need to take my wool sweater off.

12. A) set up . . . She decided to arrange an online meeting with all of her colleagues.
    B) She decided to set up an online meeting with all of her colleagues.

13. A) turn down . . . I'm cold, so could you reduce the power of the air conditioning?
    B) I'm cold, so could you turn down the air conditioning?

7.2 Answer Key

1. A) take off . . . Did you remove your shoes before entering the house?
   B) I took them off.

2. A) hand in . . . Did he give his two weeks' notice to his manager?
   B) He handed it in.

3. A) go out . . . Did they go on a date last night?
   B) They went out.

4. A) warm up . . . Did she finally get warm after walking in the snowstorm?
   B) She warmed up.

5. A) take back . . . Did he return that broken laptop to the store?
   B) He took it back.

6. A) look forward to . . . Did you expect to have fun at the party?
   B) I looked forward to it.
   /or/ I was looking forward to it.

7. A) set up . . . Did you organize that meet-and-greet event?
   B) I set it up.

8. A) drop off . . . Did you deliver those books to your friend's house?
   B) I dropped them off.

9. A) wake up . . . Did she finally awaken the kids?
   B) She woke them up.

10. A) turn down . . . Did he lower the TV volume?
    B) He turned it down.

7.3 Answer Key

1. A) plan . . . Is she going to take next Tuesday off?
   B) She plans to take it off.
   /or/ She plans to take off.

2. A) remember . . . Did he hand in his English homework?
   B) He remembered to hand it in.

3. A) want . . . Are they going to go out for drinks tonight?
   B) They want to go out.

4. A) forget . . . Did you warm up before the race?
   B) I forgot to warm up.

5. A) decide not . . . Are you going to take back those damaged headphones?
   B) I decided not to take them back.

6. A) try . . . Did you look forward to retirement?
   B) I tried to look forward to it.

7. A) promise . . . Is he going to set up more tables in the conference room?
   B) He promised to set them up.
   /or/ He promised to set some up.

8. A) agree . . . Did she drop off the paperwork at the bank?
   B) She agreed to drop it off.

9. A) try . . . Did you wake up early this morning?
   B) I tried to wake up.
   /or/ I tried to wake up early.

10. A) decide . . . Did he turn down that free flight?
    B) He decided to turn it down.

7.4 Answer Key

1. A) take off . . . They asked him to remove his baseball cap when he entered the church.
    B) Did he take it off?

2. A) hand in . . . She just finished writing her history essay, but it's too short.
    B) Is she going to hand it in?

3. A) go out . . . My coworkers wanted to go to the bars last night.
    B) Did you go out?
    /or/ Did you go out with them?

4. A) warm up . . . The kids were really cold after ice skating.
    B) Did they warm up?

5. A) take back . . . My new shoes are very uncomfortable.
    B) Are you going to take them back?

6. A) look forward to . . . She seemed excited about her presentation last week.
    B) Did she look forward to it?
    /or/ Was she looking forward to it?

7. A) set up . . . They have some great ideas for our new company website.
    B) Are they going to set it up?

8. A) drop off . . . He bought a birthday present for his grandmother.
    B) Did he drop it off?

9. A) wake up . . . I set my alarm for 3:00 a.m. yesterday.
    B) Did you wake up?

10. A) turn down . . . They have a wedding invitation, but they don't want to travel in winter.
    B) Are they going to turn it down?

8.1 Answer Key

1.   A) cool off . . . In summer, it's nice to get cool in the swimming pool.
       B) In summer, it's nice to cool off in the swimming pool.

2.   A) leave behind . . . He leaves his family in Japan when he's working abroad.
       B) He leaves his family behind in Japan when he's working abroad.

3.   A) mess up . . . She doesn't often make mistakes on tests.
       B) She doesn't often mess up on tests.
       /or/ She doesn't often mess up tests.
       /or/ She doesn't often mess tests up.

4.   A) put up . . . I place decorations in my house every December.
       B) I put up decorations in my house every December.
       /or/ I put decorations up in my house every December.

5.   A) come over . . . My friends usually come to my house on weekends.
       B) My friends usually come over on weekends.

6.   A) sign up . . . You should register for that online course.
       B) You should sign up for that online course.

7.   A) take out . . . She always asks him to carry the garbage outside.
       B) She always asks him to take out the garbage.
       /or/ She always asks him to take the garbage out.

8.   A) cheer up . . . It's easy to feel happier when the sun is shining.
       B) It's easy to cheer up when the sun is shining.

9.   A) go away . . . I hope my neighbor's big dog leaves before I go outside.
       B) I hope my neighbor's big dog goes away before I go outside.

10.   A) line up . . . Customers always stand in line outside that restaurant.
      B) Customers always line up outside that restaurant.

11.   A) leave behind . . . She always forgets her sunglasses when she goes on a trip.
      B) She always leaves her sunglasses behind when she goes on a trip.

12.   A) mess up . . . Tell the kids not to make a mess of the house while I'm gone.
      B) Tell the kids not to mess up the house while I'm gone.
      /or/ Tell the kids not to mess the house up while I'm gone.

13.   A) take out . . . He takes his daughter to a restaurant for dinner once a week.
      B) He takes his daughter out for dinner once a week.

14.   A) line up . . . I need to arrange a lot of meetings this week.
      B) I need to line up a lot of meetings this week.
      /or/ I need to line a lot of meetings up this week.

8.2 Answer Key

1.   A) cool off . . . Did the weather get cooler yesterday?
      B) It cooled off.

2.   A) leave behind . . . Did you leave your down jacket at home?
      B) I left it behind.

3.   A) mess up . . . Did the kids make a mess of the flower arrangement?
      B) They messed it up.

4.   A) put up . . . Did she display her painting on the wall?
      B) She put it up.

5.   A) come over . . . Did he arrive at your house yesterday?
      B) He came over.

6.   A) sign up . . . Did you register for those free classes?
      B) I signed up.
      /or/ I signed up for them.

7.   A) take out . . . Did she take them to a restaurant for dinner?
      B) She took them out.

8.   A) cheer up . . . Did they make her feel better?
      B) They cheered her up.

9.   A) go away . . . Did the mosquitoes disappear last week?
      B) They went away.

10.   A) line up . . . Did you arrange your job interviews for next week?
      B) I lined them up.

8.3

8.3 Answer Key

1. A) try . . . Did you cool off your dog in the shade at the park?
   B) I tried to cool him/her off.

2. A) promise . . . Is she going to leave her car behind for her daughter to use?
   B) She promised to leave it behind.

3. A) try not . . . Did she mess up her dress before the wedding?
   B) She tried not to mess it up.

4. A) decide . . . Are you going to put up those new family photos?
   B) I decided to put them up.

5. A) forget . . . Did he come over last Saturday?
   B) He forgot to come over.

6. A) plan . . . Is he going to sign up for those company English classes?
   B) He plans to sign up for them.

7. A) remember . . . Did they take the extra tables out of the conference room?
   B) They remembered to take them out.

8. A) try . . . Did she cheer up her kids last weekend when it was raining?
   B) She tried to cheer them up.

9. A) seem . . . Did the humidity go away last week?
   B) It seemed to go away.

10. A) decide not . . . Did the teacher line up her students for the fire drill?
    B) She decided not to line them up.

8.4 Answer Key

1. A) cool off . . . They were sweating a lot after their long, hot hike.
    B) Did they cool off?

2. A) leave behind . . . I can't find my umbrella, but I think I took it to work yesterday.
    B) Did you leave it behind?

3. A) mess up . . . He wasn't prepared for his driver's license test, but he decided to take it.
    B) Did he mess up?
    /or/ Did he mess it up?

4. A) put up . . . The rental company plans to deliver the wedding tent at 8:00 a.m.
    B) Are they going to put it up?

5. A) come over . . . My son's piano teacher wants to see our piano and tune it for us.
    B) Is he/she going to come over?

6. A) sign up . . . She found a great online German language course.
    B) Did she sign up?
    /or/ Did she sign up for it?

7. A) take out . . . My contacts are bothering my eyes.
    B) Are you going to take them out?

8. A) cheer up . . . They lost their baseball game, but the coach gave them a pep talk.
    B) Did he/she cheer them up?
    /or/ Did they cheer up?

9. A) go away . . . I had a headache all morning.
    B) Did it go away?

10. A) line up . . . She recommended three more artists for our art exhibition next month.
    B) Is she going to line them up?
    /or/ Did she line them up?

9.1 Answer Key

1. A) stay up . . . My kids always stay awake until midnight.
   B) My kids always stay up until midnight.

2. A) pack up . . . We should gather and pack our camping gear.
   B) We should pack up our camping gear.
   /or/ We should pack our camping gear up.

3. A) check out . . . She wants to pay the cashier before the store closes.
   B) She wants to check out before the store closes.

4. A) take down . . . I always remove my holiday decorations in January.
   B) I always take down my holiday decorations in January.
   /or/ I always take my holiday decorations down in January.

5. A) make sure . . . Can you confirm we have hotel reservations?
   B) Can you make sure we have hotel reservations?

6. A) put back . . . He told his son to place the cookies on the table again.
   B) He told his son to put the cookies back on the table.

7. A) take up . . . She plans to start learning golf when she retires.
   B) She plans to take up golf when she retires.

8. A) calm down . . . Their dog never becomes calm around new people.
   B) Their dog never calms down around new people.

9. A) get lost . . . I always lose my way in big cities.
   B) I always get lost in big cities.

10. A) hang up . . . He puts his school uniform on a hanger every night.
    B) He hangs up his school uniform every night.
    /or/ He hangs his school uniform up every night.

11. A) check out . . . I'd like to observe that private school before I enroll my daughter.
    B) I'd like to check out that private school before I enroll my daughter.
    /or/ I'd like to check that private school out before I enroll my daughter.

12. A) hang up . . . If a scammer calls you, you should end the call right away.
    B) If a scammer calls you, you should hang up right away.

9.2 Answer Key

1. A) stay up . . . Did he stay awake late last night?
    B) He stayed up.

2. A) pack up . . . Did they gather and pack the leftover food after the party?
    B) They packed it up.

3. A) check out . . . Did she go to see that new cafe?
    B) She checked it out.

4. A) take down . . . Did you dismantle your tent before leaving your campsite?
    B) I took it down.

5. A) make sure . . . Did he check and confirm that the kids are asleep?
    B) He made sure.

6. A) put back . . . Did you replace those books on the shelf when you were finished?
    B) I put them back.

7. A) take up . . . Did she start doing yoga last year?
    B) She took it up.

8. A) calm down . . . Did the kids become calm after the earthquake?
    B) They calmed down.

9. A) get lost . . . Did they lose their way at the airport?
    B) They got lost.

10. A) hang up . . . Did he end his phone call with that telemarketer?
    B) He hung up.

9.3 Answer Key

1. A) plan . . . Are they going to stay up for the midnight movie showing?
    B) They plan to stay up.
    /or/ They plan to stay up for it.

2. A) decide . . . Did he already pack up all his ski gear?
    B) He decided to pack it up.

3. A) plan . . . Are you going to check out that new apartment?
    B) I plan to check it out.

4. A) decide not . . . Did that celebrity take down his social media post?
    B) He decided not to take it down.

5. A) promise . . . Is she going to make sure your cats are okay while you're gone?
    B) She promised to make sure.

6. A) forget . . . Did they put the lawnmower back in the garage?
    B) They forgot to put it back.

7. A) hope . . . Are you going to take up piano this year?
    B) I hope to take it up.

8. A) try . . . Did he calm down his hyper kids at the restaurant?
    B) He tried to calm them down.

9. A) happen . . . Did she get lost on her way to the restaurant?
    B) She happened to get lost.

10. A) remember . . . Did you hang up the wet towels in the bathroom?
    B) I remembered to hang them up.

9.4 Answer Key

1. A) stay up . . . He planned to watch the Olympics at 1:00 a.m.
    B) Did he stay up?

2. A) pack up . . . She wants to take all her old clothes to the secondhand shop.
    B) Is she going to pack them up?
    /or/ Did she pack them up?

3. A) check out . . . My kids really want to go to that new amusement park.
    B) Are you going to check it out?
    /or/ Are they going to check it out?

4. A) take down . . . The construction crew put up roadblocks on my street last month.
    B) Did they take them down?

5. A) make sure . . . I asked him to confirm that there are vegan options at the restaurant.
    B) Did he make sure?

6. A) put back . . . I asked her to put the car in the garage after she borrowed it.
    B) Did she put it back?

7. A) take up . . . My son is crazy about surfing, but he's never tried it before.
    B) Is he going to take it up?

8. A) calm down . . . His grandkids were too excited to go to bed.
    B) Did he calm them down?
    /or/ Did they calm down?

9. A) get lost . . . I took the wrong train at Tokyo Station this morning.
    B) Did you get lost?

10. A) hang up . . . She has been on the phone with a telemarketer for the past 20 minutes.
    B) Is she going to hang up?
    /or/ Is she going to hang up on him/her/them?

10.1 Answer Key

1. A) go over . . . He always explains the instructions multiple times.
    B) He always goes over the instructions multiple times

2. A) believe in . . . Do you believe that ghosts are real?
    B) Do you believe in ghosts?

3. A) clear up . . . She resolves many issues at work.
    B) She clears up many issues at work.

4. A) shut down . . . The company stopped doing business in January.
    B) The company shut down in January.

5. A) give up . . . He wants to quit smoking.
    B) He wants to give up smoking.

6. A) move into . . . I want to start living in my new apartment soon.
    B) I want to move into my new apartment soon.

7. A) hang on . . . I'm busy, so could you wait for a moment?
    B) I'm busy, so could you hang on?
    /or/ I'm busy, so could you hang on for a moment?

8. A) put together . . . She often organizes presentations at work.
    B) She often puts together presentations at work.
    /or/ She often puts presentations together at work.

9. A) stay away from . . . I avoid dangerous areas in the city.
    B) I stay away from dangerous areas in the city.

10. A) think about . . . It's important for students to consider their future careers.
    B) It's important for students to think about their future careers.

11. A) hang onto . . . These stairs are steep, so you should keep holding the railing.
    B) These stairs are steep, so you should hang onto the railing.

12. A) believe in . . . He believes that his country's Olympic team will do well.
    B) He believes in his country's Olympic team.

13. A) clear up . . . The weather will become clear tomorrow.
    B) The weather will clear up tomorrow.

14. A) go over . . . She plans to have an editor carefully check her scientific article.
    B) She plans to have an editor go over her scientific article.

15. A) put together . . . His son loves to assemble puzzles.
    B) His son loves to put puzzles together.
    /or/ His son loves to put together puzzles.

16. A) hang onto . . . Did you decide to keep your old car for a while?
    B) Did you decide to hang onto your old car (for awhile)?

10.2 Answer Key

1.   A) go over . . . Did he examine your report?
        B) He went over it.

2.   A) believe in . . . Do they have confidence that she will become a famous musician?
        B) They believe in her.

3.   A) clear up . . . Did the sky become clear after the rain?
        B) It cleared up.

4.   A) shut down . . . Did the owner close his restaurant during Covid?
        B) He shut it down.
        /or/ He shut down.

5.   A) give up on . . . Did she stop trying to become a YouTube star?
        B) She gave up on it.

6.   A) move in . . . Did they transport all their furniture to their new house?
        B) They moved in.

7.   A) hang onto . . . Did you decide to keep your old piano?
        B) I hung onto it.

8.   A) put together . . . Did the kids assemble their new Lego set?
        B) They put it together.

9.   A) stay away from . . . Did he avoid his coworkers yesterday?
        B) He stayed away from them.

10.   A) think about . . . Did she carefully consider changing jobs?
        B) She thought about it.

10.3 Answer Key

1. A) forget . . . Did the teacher go over that recipe in cooking class?
    B) She forgot to go over it.

2. A) try . . . Did you believe in your brother's new business idea?
    B) I tried to believe in it.

3. A) hope . . . Is he going to clear up the argument between his children?
    B) He hopes to clear it up.

4. A) plan . . . Are they going to shut down their factory in Mexico?
    B) They plan to shut it down.

5. A) decide not . . . Did you give up on your dream of becoming a doctor?
    B) I decided not to give up on it.

6. A) decide . . . Is she going to move in with her parents?
    B) She decided to move in.
    /or/ She decided to move in with them.

7. A) forget . . . Did you hang onto your old school yearbooks?
    B) I forgot to hang onto them.

8. A) want . . . Is she going to put that Ikea shelf together?
    B) She wants to put it together.

9. A) promise . . . Did the kids stay away from the park last night?
    B) They promised to stay away.
    /or/ They promised to stay away from there.
    /or/ They promised to stay away from it.

10. A) refuse . . . Did he think about moving back to California?
    B) He refused to think about it.

10.4 Answer Key

1. A) go over . . . I asked him to check my PowerPoint presentation for mistakes.
    B) Did he go over it?

2. A) believe in . . . When I was a kid, my brother told me that vampires are real.
    B) Did you believe in them?
    /or/ Did he believe in them?

3. A) clear up . . . My boss says she will explain our confusing new remote-work policy.
    B) Is she going to clear it up?

4. A) shut down . . . The rail company was worried about running trains during the storm.
    B) Did they shut them down?
    /or/ Did it shut them down?

5. A) give up . . . He thinks eating red meat is unhealthy and bad for the environment.
    B) Is he going to give it up?
    /or/ Did he give it up?

6. A) move into . . . Her company gave her a big, private office.
    B) Did she move into it?

7. A) hang onto . . . I was walking my dog, and he tried to chase a stray cat.
    B) Did you hang onto him?

8. A) put together . . . My neighbor bought a new gas grill, but she hasn't assembled it yet.
    B) Is she going to put it together?

9. A) stay away . . . His in-laws told him not to visit, because they had the flu.
    B) Did he stay away?

10. A) think about . . . Her company wants her to move to New York City.
    B) Is she going to think about it?

Index